ARMY GUIDE TO SEOUL+

YouGen Media
Los Angeles California
Seoul, South Korea
www.yougenmedia.com

This publication is designed to provide accurate and authoritative information in regard to the subject matter covered. While YouGen Media has used their best efforts in preparing this book, they make no representations or warranties with respect to the accuracy or completeness of the contents of this book. Neither the publisher nor the author shall be liable for any loss of profit or any other commercial damages, including but not limited to special, incidental, consequential, personal, or other damages.

Written by Bora K, Jennifer Roe, and Ha Eun-Hee
Designed by Sanghwa Lee
Photography by Matthew Ha, Jennifer Roe
Maps by Sanghwa Lee

ISBN: 979-8-9895246-0-0

First edition 2023

For
Kim Namjoon, Kim Seok-Jin, Min Yoongi,
Jung Hoseok, Park Jimin, Kim Taehyung,
Jeon Jungkook - BTS

&

All the **A**dorable **R**epresentative **M**.C. for **Y**outh out there

Table of Contents

Weekend Trip

Introductions

From the Editor

As a Korean-American, I was exposed to Korean Culture, or K-Culture, from my earliest memory. Growing up in the 'melting pot' of American culture, it was first at home through my mother who spoke to me in Korean and made Korean food. Nearly every family meal had at least kimchi as banchan (side dish) but often a chigae (soup) to accompany a bowl of rice 밥 (bab - the Korean for rice which is synonymous for meal). But as many teenagers can attest, I wanted to fit in and be like my other 'American' friends and didn't want to appear weird or different, so I spoke to my mother in English and preferred a bowl of cereal to rice for breakfast. Since I grew up in the suburbs with little access to the likes of Koreatown in LA or NYC, it was easy enough for me to assimilate. Fast forward to university when I left home and missed my mother and was trying to figure out who I was and what I wanted to do with

my life. I found myself wanting to know more about my heritage and the more I learned about Korean history, the more I got to understand my parents and the sacrifices they made as immigrants in a foreign land.

In 2018, I heard a song which I was surprised to learn was K-pop. Like many ARMY, BTS came to me when I needed them most. Like a warm embrace, Love Yourself: Answer gave me refuge. That the songs were sung in Korean and English made me feel as if they were intended just for me. BTS propelled me to discover myself and not to hide from pain but to confront it. For me, what is beautiful about this group of 7 members of a K-pop band is that they somehow bring to the world the best of what it means to be human: to love, to hurt and to find good in humanity.

As I arrived in Korea to continue this discovery of Korean culture and history, I met countless ARMY who had also come to Korea to pursue a curiosity that was both personal and universal. What I found was that so many were in a new country eager to go to places that reminded them of BTS but were hampered by their lack of Korean or lack of infrastructure to support their kind of tourism. How many tourists have gone to Gangneung trying to find the bus stop from the Wings album cover only to be stranded because the buses only ran occasionally? After hearing horror stories from Korean taxi drivers and ARMY alike, this guide is my way of helping. A percentage of profits can fund various ARMY causes. If you are reading this, I thank you for your contribution to this effort. - Ha Eun Hee 하은희

From the Author

Finding the right words to introduce this project has taken me much longer than I anticipated. In a way, the reason for making this little book is quite simple: out of love for BTS.

Yet the longer I worked on this and the more places I visited, the more I began to understand that it is something deeper than that. As I was returning from dinner at one of the restaurants listed in this book, I suddenly remembered what RM said during a concert. I don't remember the exact quote, but it went along the lines of: "You all knew us at different times, it could be 4 years ago or 3 years ago, or 1 year ago. And I think that moment was the beginning. I hope that that is when your beautiful moment began."

I think about this quote a lot because I, like many ARMY, did not discover BTS right after they debuted in 2013. But I know that for me personally, a very happy time began from the moment I did get to know them and the community of ARMY that is always surrounding them. I found their music at a time of uncertainty in my life in which I was questioning all my decisions and was plagued with anxieties about my future, at the age of 22! The world seemed too big to tackle and

I found myself turning to these 7 boys whose music helped me relieve some of those anxieties and fears and led me into a community full of people who understood what I was going through.

In compiling and visiting all of these places, I got to relive some of my favorite memories with BTS and got to reflect on what it was that made me fall in love with their music and how they changed me. In a way, it was not merely a walk down BTS's memory lane but also my own. I would visit the set of a specific Run BTS! episode and remember what I was going through at the time I first saw that episode and how it cheered me up, certain lyrics would feel much different than when I first heard them, the feelings I had when I first watched a music video, and the feelings I felt years later standing on the actual set for that music video. I got to remember all the beautiful people and places that I have seen along the way and it helped me personally to reflect on myself and who I am.

Either way, it is supposed to make you feel connected to the boys in a different way while discovering their beautiful country and its culture. It does not matter when you discovered BTS, whether your memories date back to 2013 or have been created last month, the year that this book is being made in. You may have a special connection to one of their songs, performances, music videos or other content, like Run BTS! This book aims to make you experience those events in an even more memorable way and make new memories to connect with the pre-existing ones.

In a way, that is all this book is: a collection of memories.

It includes restaurants, cafés, museums, nature, and other kinds of locations to bring both BTS and Korea closer to you. As you may know from watching BTS, food is one of the most important aspects of Korean culture. The members, much like the majority of Koreans, love to admire nature and drinking Iced Americanos. Through you will not only get a taste of Korea, but also get to discover its history and culture.

My wish for you is that this book will help you make experiences that can become beautiful memories and to help you connect with BTS in your own unique way.
-BK 보라

Before Coming to Korea

Each country has different travel regulations. Please double check requirements before your trip. Here are some things that are worth keeping in mind.

K-ETA: If you plan on coming to Korea, you may need a K-ETA (Korea Electronic Travel Authorization). You need to get your K-ETA application approved before boarding your plane or ship, so make sure not to leave this until the last minute. You can apply on their official website. The application fee is 10,000 KRW per person. They also have an FAQ section in case you have more specific questions regarding your specific visa situation. As of April 1, 2023 Korea has created a 'Visit Korea Year 2023-2024" program in which 22 countries are temporarily exempted from requiring K-ETA visas. Refer to the K-ETA website to see if your country is exempt or not.

Currency: In Korea, they use the Korean Won (₩). They do accept overseas credit cards, but sometimes they may not work, so it is suggested you always carry some cash on you. There are a lot of ATMs where you can pick up money with foreign cards too, so if you forgot to prepare local cash in advance, or run out of it, you can always pick up more. Be careful of the fees, some banks charge more than others. Alternatively, you can exchange money at the currency exchange office either at the airport or in Seoul. They are mostly located in the Myeongdong area.

Phone/Sim card: A phone is the most useful tool while traveling around Korea as it provides maps to navigate with and ways to translate menus and signs. While free wifi is easily accessible in Seoul, it's safest to have mobile data. There are various companies that offer 90 day sim cards to tourists, such as Trazy.com, Klook or koreainfo.kr. You can get deals with call & data, data only, or rechargeable sim cards, as well as mobile wifi for daily rental or by contract, or smartphone rental and postpaid plans. It's possible to get a sim card at the airport without prior reservation, but to avoid unexpected issues, it is best to reserve the product beforehand and pick them up at the airport upon arrival.

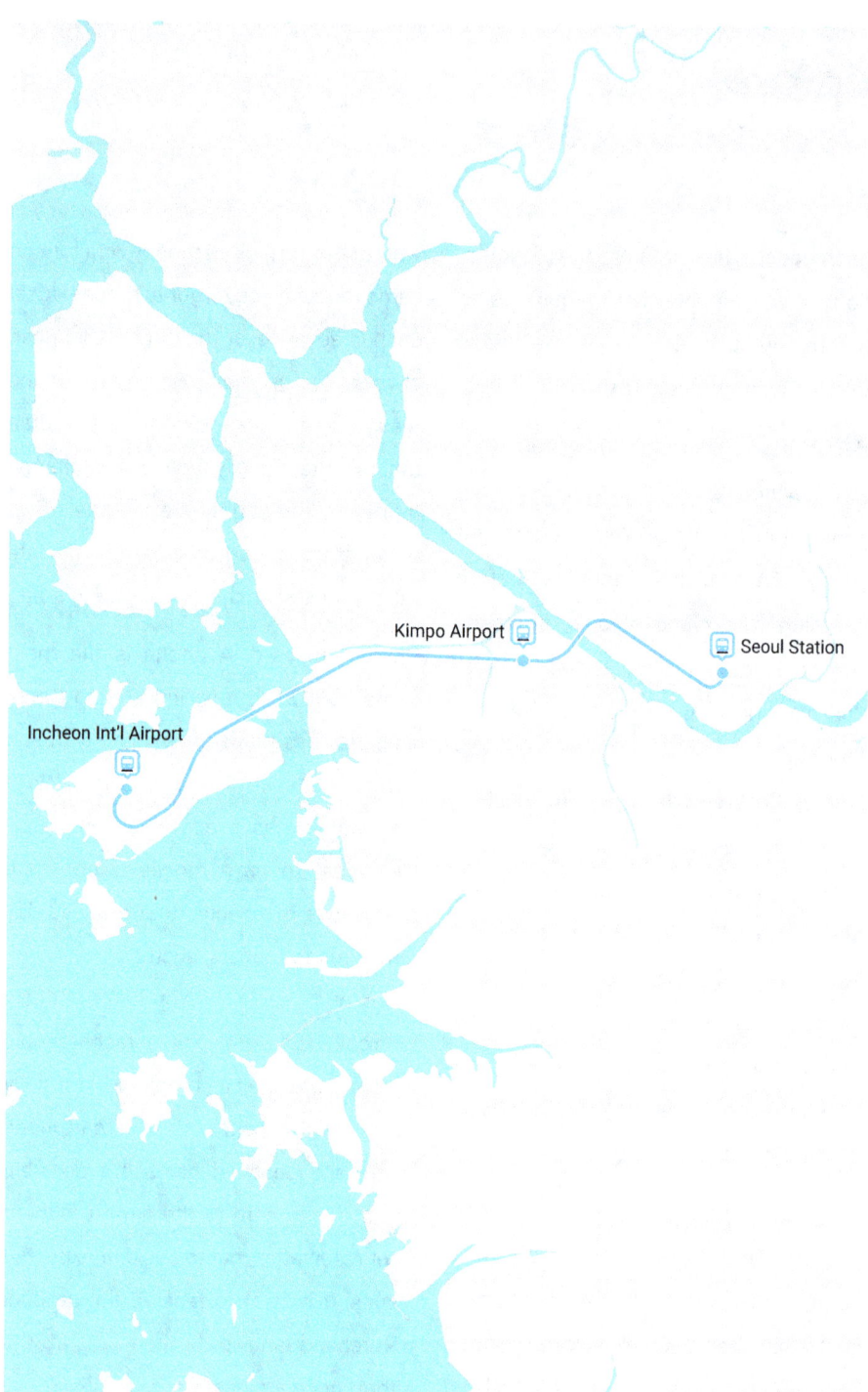

How to Get There

You will most likely arrive at Incheon International Airport, which is approximately 50 km (31 miles) away from Seoul. It is recommended to download either 'Kakao Maps' or 'Naver Maps,' as those are the two most reliable navigation apps for South Korea. They will also be useful later on when navigating through Seoul. These apps will give you several public transport, taxi, and walking options for your destinations. Public transportation is very well organized and easy to understand and most stops are announced and displayed in English, too.

To get to Seoul from Incheon International Airport, there are several options available: taxi, bus, and train. The taxi is pretty self-explanatory, it is only worth keeping in mind that Uber is not common in Korea. Kakao Taxi is the most popular taxi service. There are several types of taxis, such as standard, international, deluxe, and vans. They vary according to the size and service they provide, with international taxi drivers speaking English, Japanese or Chinese. If you take a limousine bus from the airport, you can either buy a ticket at the automated kiosk machines, which are available in English, or purchase a ticket at the ticket booth.

As for the AREX (Airport Express) train, you can either buy a single ticket or buy a T-Money card right away. A T-Money card is most recommended. It's a rechargeable public transportation card that can be used throughout all of Korea for buses, taxis and the subway. It is the most convenient way to navigate public transport. If you do not get a T-Money card at the airport, you can purchase them in most convenience stores and subway stations. To recharge them, you can do so in cash only, either on the machines in subway stations or in convenience stores.

TMONEY

Things to Know
꿀팁:

There are a couple of things that you should know when coming to Korea. These include some technical details that are worth keeping in mind, but also cultural and behavioral aspects. Since ARMY is representative of BTS and you will be visiting a lot of places related to them, it's important not to make certain faux pas because it might reflect badly on the fandom and the group. Some cultural differences might leave you puzzled, so important ones were noted to help you avoid confusion on either side.

Birthday Events: In Korea, it is common for fans of all kinds of groups and artists to organize various birthday events for their favorite groups or members. If you decide to come to Korea around the time of one of the members' birthdays, you can expect a very special experience. One of the most common are cupholder events that are hosted in cafés. For these, the cafés usually offer special sets with drinks and desserts that come with a variety of freebies, and the interior is decorated with balloons and photos of the members to give a festive atmosphere. They are perfect to recharge your energy on a busy day, take some cute photos, and make for nice opportunities to meet and connect with a lot of like-minded people. These birthday sets can be quite expensive, so if you can't afford to go to a lot of café events, there are always a lot of banners, billboards, or outside events to enjoy for free. You'll be surprised at how many corners these lovely birthday advertisements await you.

Another popular thing are birthday projects, such as the creation of forests dedicated to the members that are usually funded by fans and sometimes even created by volunteering fans on site.

For more information on how to find these events and prepare beforehand, check out the Birthday Event section (see page 170).

Good Deals: Some websites offer special tickets and packages specifically for foreigners who visit Seoul. If you want to visit places such as Lotte World, you can book your tickets through one of those websites, as they are cheaper and/or you might get a good package deal. Klook (klook.com) or Trazy (trazy.com) are the most well known.

Restaurants: Many restaurants specialize in one dish or type of food (for example, a restaurant only serving traditional Korean dishes), so the menu may only be that one dish but in a couple of different variations. It is a good idea to decide on the kind of food to eat beforehand or check the restaurant menu either online or outside before sitting down. It is also worth keeping in mind that many Korean dishes are designed to be shared.

Usually in restaurants customers don't wait for the waiter to come to the table and take the order. You will either have a little bell button on the table to call them, or you have to yell to call them over. Be careful with the gestures you might make while calling them over, since some gestures that are normal in other parts of the world can be considered rude in Korea.

In Korean culture, mealtime is a communal affair where food is usually served from one bowl or platter to be shared. There will also be free side dishes that can be refilled for no cost. At some restaurants there are 'self-service stations' where you collect your free water and side dishes yourself and can top them up as often as you like. These areas usually have a sign, but you can ask the staff too.

When you are done, just get up and walk straight to the counter to pay whenever you are done. While handing over your money or your credit card, always hand it over with your two hands. That is a sign of respect.

Another important thing in Korea is that you don't tip!

Public Transport: Since there are so many people living in Korea, it is important to be considerate of others at all times. For that reason, there's a social etiquette in public transportation that most people stick to. For example, you don't consume any food or drinks in the bus or subway (except for water). Another tip is to avoid having loud conversations with your friends while taking public transport. You will notice it is usually silent in the buses and subways, so as to not bother the people that may have had a really long day and want to take a rest on their way home. When you're riding a bus or subway, you may also notice a lot of people standing up even though there are free seats. Those are the seats reserved for the elderly and pregnant people. In other countries, you can just sit down and offer it to someone who needs it once they get in, but in Korea, those seats are kept free even if there is currently nobody who needs them. If you're traveling with a large backpack around rush hour, you should take it off and either put it on the floor or put it on the other way around so it's at your front. Although these are all small things, they are greatly appreciated.

General tips

If you happen to meet up with Koreans who are older, make sure you stand up to greet them. It's considered rude if you remain seated. If you're having drinks with an older Korean, you should cover your glass with your left hand and turn your head to the right while taking a sip.

Sometimes, the spice of the food might give you a runny nose, making you want to blow it. In that case, it's best to get up and go to the bathroom because blowing your nose at the table can be seen as indecent.

Smoking laws in Korea are quite strict too. There are a lot of areas where smoking is not permitted, especially the areas around subway stations and bus stops. You're also not allowed to smoke while walking. If you get caught breaking the rules, you may get fined so be careful to always check your surroundings before smoking.

Be wary of overly friendly people approaching you in the streets offering gifts or making promises to show you cool places or help you experience traditional Korean events. Though it is rare, there have been reports of foreigners being approached by aggressive Christian groups. It's best to politely decline and leave, no matter how nice they may seem.

How to Use this Guide

There are various ways this guide can help you organize a trip to Korea. The guide is divided into neighborhoods, allowing for travelers to explore area by area. It is also possible to work through the guide by categories, since most of these locations were taken from Run BTS! episodes, the members' social media posts (SNS), or other officially released videos. You can pick the desired category, identified by a hashtag, such as a specific photoshoot or landmark, and discover the respective location.

Additionally, there are 1 day, 2 day and 4 day itineraries curated to highlight the 'must see' BTS locations both in Seoul and various cities around Korea. There are day trips to cities outside of Seoul such as Ilsan, Daegu and locations including Everland and the In The Soop houses. For those with a bit more time, there are weekend trips to Gangneung, Gwangju and Busan as well.

Also included in this guide are all the venues in Seoul where BTS have performed so far. Even though access inside some of these spots are difficult, when possible at all, they are added to give an element of history to this guide and to help visitors imagine what it feels like to travel to Seoul for a concert. BTS love performing for ARMY and always work hard to put on the best show possible. Including these venues for BTS honors the hard work and creativity that they put into their shows and provides perspective of how they have grown as artists over the years. These are places where BTS and ARMY shared some of the most intimate moments with each other and created beautiful memories that are still vividly remembered by a big part of the fandom, even if they did not attend the shows themselves. The goal is to preserve these memories in this guide.

History/Timeline: Important Dates

2013

06.12.2013   2 COOL 4 SKOOL

06.13.2013   Debut date

07.09.2013   ARMY birthday

09.03.2013   First episode of Rookie King

09.11.2013   O!RUL8,2?

11.14.2013   Best New Artist (Rookie of the Year) at Melon Music Awards

2014

02.12.2014   Skool Luv Affair

05.14.2014   Skool Luv Affair (Repackage)

07.24.2014   First episode of American Hustle Life

08.20.2014   Dark & Wild

12.24.2014   Wake Up (Japanese Studio Album)

2014   First concert tour "The Red Bullet Tour"

2015

04.29.2015   The Most Beautiful Moment in Life Pt. 1

05.05.2015   "I NEED U" First music show win on SBS MTV's "The Show"

08.01.2015   First episode of Run BTS!

08.11.2015   First episode of BTS Gayo

11.30.2015   The Most Beautiful Moment in Life Pt. 2

2016

05.02.2016   The Most Beautiful Moment in Life: Young Forever

07.05.2016   First episode of Bon Voyage

09.07.2016   Youth (Japanese Full Album)

10.10.2016 Wings

11.19.2016 BTS win first Daesang (Grand Prize) Best Album of the Year at MMA for The Most Beautiful Moment in Life: Young Forever

2017

02.13.2017 You Never Walk Alone

05.21.2017 Top Social Artist award at the 24th Billboard Music Awards

11.18.2017 Love Yourself: Her

11.19.2017 Performs U.S. TV debut at American Music Awards (DNA)

2018

04.04.2018 Face Yourself (Japanese Studio Album)

05.18.2018 Love Yourself: Tear

05.24.2018 BTS first debut no. 1 on Billboard 200 Album charts

08.24.2018 Love Yourself: Answer

09.24.2018 First speech at the United Nations

10.24.2018 Awarded Order of Cultural Merit by South Korean Government

2019

02.10.2019 Attends 61st Grammy Awards as award presenters

04.12.2019 Map of the Soul: Persona

04.29.2019 Named among the 100 most influential people of the year by Time magazine

06.28.2019 BTS World: Original Soundtrack

2019 First Stadium World Tour "BTS World Tour: Love Yourself"

2020

02.21.2020 Map of the Soul: 7

07.14.2020 Map of the Soul: 7 ~The Journey~ (Japanese Studio Album)

08.19.2020 First episode of In The Soop

08.21.2020 Dynamite (English Single)

09.25.2020 BTS first debut no. 1 Billboard Top 100 chart for "Dynamite"

| 11.20.2020 | BE |
| 11.25.2020 | First Grammy nomination for "Dynamite" |

2021

03.14.2021	First Korean nominee to perform their song at 63rd Grammy Awards
05.21.2021	Butter (English Single)
06.16.2021	BTS, THE BEST (Japanese Compilation Album)
09.14.2021	Appointed special envoy by President Moon Jae-in ahead of 78th U.N. General Assembly
10.15.2021	First episode In The Soop Season 2
11.23.2021	Second Grammy nomination for "Butter"
07.09.2021	Permission to Dance (English Single)

2022

04.03.2022	Performs "Butter" at the 64th Grammy Awards
05.31.2022	Visit to the White House
06.10.2022	Proof
06.14.2022	Announcement of temporary break during Festa dinner
07.15.2022	Jack in The Box (j-hope Solo Album)
07.19.2022	World Expo 2030 Busan bid announces BTS as official ambassadors
07.31.2022	j-hope headlining act Lollapalooza in Chicago (Solo Debut)
10.15.2022	BTS Yet To Come free concert in Busan for World Expo 2030 Busan
10.17.2022	Big Hit announces all members will fulfill military enlistment
11.15.2022	Third Grammy nomination for "Yet To Come MV" and "My Universe"
11.20.2022	Dreamers by Jung Kook feat. Fahad Al Kubaisi released as FIFA World Cup 2022 Qatar Official Soundtrack (Solo Single)
11.20.2022	Jung Kook performs at FIFA World Cup 2022 with Fahad Al Kubaisi
10.28.2022	Astronaut by Jin (Solo Single)
10.28.2022	Jin performs "Astronaut" at Coldplay's Stadium Concert in Argentina (Solo Debut)
12.02.2022	Indigo (RM Solo Album)

12.05.2022	RM live solo concert at Rolling Hall (Solo Debut)
12.05.2022	First episode of Suchwita
12.13.2022	Jin enlists in South Korean military
12.31.2022	j-hope performs live for 'Dick Clark's New Year's Rockin' Eve' in NYC

2023

02.17.2023	j-hope IN THE BOX documentary on Disney+
03.03.2023	On the Street by j-hope with J. Cole (Solo Single)
03.24.2023	Face (Jimin Solo Album)
03.24.2023	Jimin performs on The Tonight Show Starring Jimmy Fallon (US Solo Debut)
04.18.2023	j-hope enlists in South Korean military
04.21.2023	D-Day (SUGA/Agust D Solo Album)
04.21.2023	SUGA: Road to D-Day documentary on Disney+
04.26.2023	SUGA Agust D Tour (Solo Debut)
05.01.2023	SUGA performs on The Tonight Show Starring Jimmy Fallon (US Solo Debut)
06.13.2023	Take Two (Single)
06.13.2023	BTS 10 year anniversary
06.17.2023	BTS 10th anniversary festival held in Yeouido Han River Park
07.14.2023	Seven by Jung Kook (Solo Debut Single)
07.14.2023	Jung Kook performs on Good Morning America's Summer concert series (US Solo Debut)
09.08.2023	Layover (V Solo Album)
09.22.2023	SUGA enlists in South Korean military
09.23.2023	Jung Kook performs solo set at Global Citizen Festival in NYC
09.23.2023	3D by Jung Kook with Jack Harlow (Solo Single)
10.14.2023	V hosts his fanmeeting 'Vicnic' with surprise guest Jumin
11.03.2023	Golden (Jung Kook Solo Album)
11.20.2023	Jung Kook hosts [GOLDEN] Live On Stage

Terminology: How to speak BTS

Agust D: SUGA's stage name for solo projects.

ARMY: The name of the fandom is an abbreviation of 'Adorable Representative M.C. for Youth.' Fun fact: in July 2021 the members told Jimmy Fallon in an interview that initially they were going to name the fandom 'Bells' because of the similarity between the 'bang' in the Korean word for bell 'bangwool' (방울) and their Korean name 'bangtansonyeondan.'

Armybomb: This is the name of the group's lightstick. It has a concert mode that connects through bluetooth and makes them part of the show. As most K-Pop groups have their own lightsticks, they're also helpful during big events with multiple fandoms so they can spot their fans in the crowd.

Bang PD: Also known as 'Hitman Bang', his real name is Bang Si-Hyuk and he is the founder and chairman of HYBE (formerly BigHit Entertainment).

Bias: One's favorite member of the group.

Bias wrecker: That one member that makes one question their initial bias choice.

BigHit: The entertainment company that manages BTS. Formerly BigHit Entertainment, it was rebranded as BigHit Music, a subsidiary under the parent company HYBE Corporation.

Birthday Events: Events, billboards, advertisements, projects, installations, etc organized for the members' birthdays or the group's anniversary.

Bon Voyage: A travel show in which the boys travel around the world and visit/discover. The show started in 2016 and is available on Weverse (contrary to Run BTS!, you have to pay to watch Bon Voyage).

Borahae: From the Korean "보라해", literally translated, "I purple you." It is used both by the members and ARMY to say "I love you."

BTS: A lot of people associate the letters BTS with 'Behind the Scenes,' but the name BTS actually stands for 'Bulletproof Boy Scouts,' or in Korean, 'Bangtan Sonyeondan.' (방탄소년단).

......

BTS Universe / BU: A fictional story that was started in 2015 and was created through music videos, notes in the physical albums, and was later expanded into mobile games, webtoons, books, etc.

......

BT21: A collaboration between BTS and Line Friends in which each member got to design their own character. RM created Koya, the blue koala while Jin created RJ, the white alpaca. SUGA created Shooky, the brown cookie and j-hope created Mang, who started as blue and wearing a pony-mask but in 2023 was unmasked to be a purple squirrel. Jimin created Chimmy, the yellow dog, whereas V created Tata, the red heart-shaped alien and Jung Kook created Cooky, the pink muscle bunny. There is also Van, a giant space robot that is meant to represent ARMY who is the protector.

......

Comeback: Although in a Western understanding this word implies that an artist has been gone for a longer time, in the K-pop world it is equivalent to 'putting out new music.'

......

Dance Practice: A high quality video usually taken inside the practice studio that shows them dancing/practicing the choreography of a song. Unlike in music videos or live performances where the editing makes it hard to see the whole choreo, dance practices let you focus on all the important aspects of the choreography.

......

Date format: The date is usually formatted as YYMMDD. This format is often used by fans for fancams, photos, or just to refer to important dates. Official performance videos also often use this date format. BTS's debut date is usually written as 130613.

......

Debut: The date or song that marks the beginning of a group's activities. For BTS, the debut date is June 13th 2013 and their debut song was "No More Dream."

......

Fancam: The more members a group has, the harder it is to focus on one specific member. A fancam refers to a video that focuses on one specific member for the entire performance.

......

Fanchant: The chant that fans recite during live performances. It usually consists of the members' names and the group's name. For example, BTS's fanchant is: Kim Namjoon, Kim Seokjin, Min Yoongi, Jung Hoseok, Park Jimin, Kim Taehyung, Jeon Jungkook, BTS. (For the fanchant, their real names are used. It starts with RM, the leader, then goes in order of oldest to youngest).

Fansite: This term usually refers to a fan that follows the group on their official schedules to take pictures of a specific member (for example, a j-hope fansite will take photos only of j-hope and a SUGA fansite will take photos only of SUGA, etc). Those official schedules can include concerts and performances, but also appearances in other public spaces, such as airports. It is also these fansites that usually organize the birthday events and projects. In fact, most of the photos used for these birthday advertisements or for decoration and goodies at cafés are photos that these fansites took themselves. Sometimes the projects are funded by the profit made by selling their own goods, such as slogans and banners or keychains.

While most fansites respect the group's privacy, in recent years there have been multiple fansites that were found to violate these privacy rules, following the boys on unofficial schedules and engaging in stalking behavior. In 2019, BigHit even released a public list of fansites that they found were violating fansite etiquette and engaged in unacceptable behavior (invasion of privacy, illegal photography, etc), blacklisting them from all future events and places that BTS would attend. This also raised concerns and debates among other fans as to how much support should be given to these fansites and their events/projects, for fear that they will encourage and enable more of this unacceptable behavior.

Festa: An anniversary celebration in June that stretches itself over an extended period of time, in which they release new dance practices, surprise songs, unreleased photos, and other types of content. It varies year by year.

HYBE: HYBE Corporation is an entertainment company that was started by Bang PD as BigHit Entertainment in 2005 and was rebranded in 2021.

Hyung line: Hyung (형) refers to the oldest of a group (here Jin). If you refer to all the older members, you call them the Hyung line: Jin, SUGA, j-hope, and RM. RM is often referred to as the 'Maknae of the Hyung line', as he is the youngest of the oldest.

HYYH: Also known as the "HYYH" era, an acronym for the Korean name Hwa Yang Yeon Hwa (화양연화), this BTS period was defined by three thematically linked musical releases. BTS's third EP, The Most Beautiful Moment in Life, Pt.1, their fourth EP, The Most Beautiful Moment in Life, Pt. 2, and their first compilation album, The Most Beautiful Moment in Life: Young Forever. BTS's second Japanese studio album, Youth, is also considered as part of their HYYH era along with their Japanese singles "For You," "I NEED U" and "Run."

In The Soop: A reality series that was broadcasted on national television (JTBC), as well as Weverse. It features the boys taking a break from their busy lives to relax and enjoy different activities and hobbies. The first season was filmed in a remote area in Chuncheon by a lake, while the second season took place in a villa in the mountains. There is a third season that only includes V and his friends group, called Friendcation as opposed to 'staycation.'

Maknae line: Maknae (막내) refers to the youngest of a group (in this case Jung Kook). If you refer to all the younger members, you call them the Maknae line: Jimin, V, and Jung Kook.

Mixtape: A member's solo work often self-produced that has no physical albums or sales. These mixtapes were posted for free and without fanfare on various platforms. Following the success of the mixtapes, the rapline and vocal line

have made solo albums which include physical albums and sales.

Muster: The name of BTS's fan gatherings. It's an event where they perform songs but also play games. 'Muster' is a military term that refers to the gathering of troops, so in this case it's a gathering of ARMY. It often happens within the Festa period.

MV: Short form for 'music video.'

Photocard: Random, individual photos of the members that usually come with albums, DVDs, and other merch. People like to collect photocards of their bias.

Rapline: A term in K-Pop used to refer to the three rappers of the group. Ours are RM, SUGA, and j-hope.

Run BTS! 달려라 방탄: This is the name of BTS's web variety show, in which they play various games. The show was broadcasted weekly, on Tuesdays at 9PM KST. They're available for free on Weverse and YouTube.

Season's Greetings: An annual merch package that consists of calendars and year planners, usually released sometime in December. It is accompanied with a behind-the-scenes DVD.

Selca: The Korean word for selfie (셀카), from the word 'self camera.' ARMY also created 'Army Selca Day' where they recreate the members' photos (often at the same location) and put them side by side with the original.

Stage name: Most of the members have stage names. In this book they will be referred to by their stage names, but for reference: RM = Kim Namjoon, Jin = Kim Seokjin, SUGA = Min Yoongi, j-hope = Jung Hoseok, Jimin = Park Jimin, V = Kim Taehyung, Jung Kook = Jeon Jungkook.

Stan: A word that means 'fan' or 'to be a fan of something.' For example: I stan BTS, or, I am a BTS stan. It can also have a negative connotation to refer to more 'extreme' fans, for example when someone is referred to as a 'solo stan' which is looked down upon for many nuanced reasons.

SNS: Abbreviation for 'Social Networking Service.' It includes social media platforms such as Twitter, Instagram, and Weverse.

Sub-unit: Sometimes not all members are featured on a song. The selection of specific members on songs is called a 'sub-unit.' For example, the '3J' sub-unit is a dance focused group including j-hope, Jimin and Jung Kook.

Summer Package: Another merch package similar to Season's Greetings. Usually consists of some gadget, a behind the scenes DVD, a photobook, and posters.

Vocal line: A term used to refer to the four vocalists of the group: Jin, Jimin, V, and Jung Kook.

Vlive: A live video streaming platform that was used by the members to do livestreams and to distribute content such as comeback trailers, Run BTS!, Bon Voyage, etc. Vlive unified with Weverse in 2023 and so all content and livestreams take place on Weverse now.

Weverse: A fan community app created by HYBE, made for artists and fans to interact (uploading posts, commenting, sharing stories) but also to distribute membership only content, music videos, Bon Voyage, Run BTS!, etc.

Winter Package: The same as Summer Package, except they switched to a different season.

Itineraries

1 Day in Seoul

9 am: Gyeongbokgung (see page 146)

Gyeongbokgung palace is an attraction that you wouldn't want to miss when you visit Seoul.

The beautiful and traditional architecture of the palace offers an insight into the country's history, but also gives you beautiful photo opportunities. You can take a stroll through the spacious palace complex to see the various buildings, ponds, and people dressed in traditional clothes. If you want to, you can even wear a hanbok yourself, in which case you get in the palace for free. (You can rent a hanbok in the stores near the palace).

Another highlight of Gyeongbokgung palace is the 'changing of guards.' This ceremony dates back to the Joseon dynasty when the royal guards guarded the palace gates. If you want to see

a traditional scene that also involves traditional Korean instruments, make sure to be there at either 10am or 2pm (keep in mind that the palace is closed on Tuesdays) and try to arrive a bit in advance to secure a good viewing spot. The duration of the performance is approximately 20 minutes.

If during your exploration of Gyeongbokgung you feel like some of the locations are familiar, then you're right. BTS's iconic "Idol" and "Mikrokosmos" performances on Jimmy Fallon were shot here. They also did a special performance of "Dynamite" at the Geunjeongjeon Grand Residence which they released as a Bangtan Bomb in October 2020.

11 am: Bukchon Hanok Village

Take a stroll through Bukchon Hanok Village, a Korean traditional village situated in Seoul on the top of the hill between Gyeongbokgung Palace and Changdeokgung Palace. It is a residential area with well preserved hanoks (traditional Korean house) and narrow alleyways. Don't be surprised if you see tourists and locals dressed in hanboks, looking for photo spots. It's the perfect place to immerse yourself in Korean culture.

---

1 pm: Myeongdong

A very popular destination among tourists from all over the world is Myeongdong. Not only is this district famous for its variety in street food, cafes and restaurants in general, Myeongdong also has the largest concentration of cosmetic shops in Seoul. The countless stores and their skincare brands are endorsed by the most popular idols and BTS is no exception.

If you are looking for inexpensive K-Pop related souvenirs, you shouldn't miss Myeongdong Underground Mall directly connected to Myeongdong Station. Both official and unofficial pieces of merch can be found in numerous stores and prices are generally low. From lightsticks to albums, unofficial photocards to calendars, you'll find everything your K-Pop heart desires in this neighborhood.

---

3 pm: For the heart and for the S(e)oul: Namsan Tower and Namsan Park

One of the most popular attractions in Yongsan and all of Seoul is Namsan. On the top of Namsan Mountain you get not only a stunning view over Seoul, but you can also discover interesting landmarks such as N Seoul Tower (also referred to as Namsan Tower) , a variety of hiking trails and the setting for numerous K-Dramas and movies. The cable car (close to Myeongdong Station exit 4) is also popular amongst Namsan's visitors. It is a unique way to ascend or descend Namsan. You can also buy a lock and put it on the designated 'locks of love' area to create unforgettable memories.

---

5 pm: Museum date: HYBE Headquarters/National Museum of Korea (see page 119/114)

A must see for every ARMY is the HYBE headquarters and location of the original HYBE Insight museum located in Yongsan-gu. The eye-catching modern glass building on the main road of Yongsan's business district used to host a museum and exhibition space on the two basement floors. It was created especially for ARMY but also for fans of other HYBE artists, such as TOMORROW X TOGETHER, ENHYPEN, and Seventeen (to name only a few). Since January 2023 HYBE Insight has been closed, but it is still a great photo spot. Cafe Black Drum, an elaborately decorated BTS fan cafe all-year round, is located behind HYBE and adds to the experience of visiting where BTS work.

If you prefer history over modern art, you can alternatively visit the impressive National Museum of Korea, which is located in the same area as HYBE. It is the largest museum in Korea and is the perfect place to expand your knowledge about Korea's history. Through the numerous galleries that display Korea's most important relics from 2000 years, you can get a glimpse into the country's rich history. This museum is also where BTS gave their "Dear Class of 2020" speech and performed "Boy With Luv," "Spring Day" and "Mikrokosmos." The museum itself is worth a visit, but even if you don't want to go inside, you can just stroll around the outdoor area. It has a beautiful pond and park area which offers a wonderful view of N Seoul Tower.

Located right next to the National Museum of Korea is the National Hangeul Museum. This museum is dedicated to the creation, development and principles behind Korea's unique alphabet and writing system. The Korean Hangeul is the only writing system that has been completely documented since its creation by King Sejong. The exhibit is very engaging and can be explored properly within an hour or so, making it a great addition to your itinerary list while in the area.

---

7 pm: Eat dinner like a K-Pop Rookie

Make your way to the Gangnam area where a lot of other interesting BTS-related locations are waiting for you. Why don't you have Korean food at Yoojung restaurant (see page 46) for the ultimate BTS experience? This is the place BTS often visited during their trainee days and the restaurant does not try to hide that: posters and pictures of the 7 men are plastered all over the walls and ceiling. The friendly staff most likely will give you one or two goodies along with your meal and the whole atmosphere will make this an unforgettable experience. Right around the corner, only a few minutes away by foot you can also spot the building where their first dormitory (see page 42) was, as well as the very first BigHit office (see page 45).

---

8 pm: K-Star Road (see page 40)

Walk off your meal by taking a stroll along the K-Star road. The K-Star road, located in the crossroads of Cheongdam and Apgujeong Rodeo, features a variety of high end luxury brands, as well as many of the entertainment agencies. That's why it's known as the road 'where stars are born.'

While walking along the streets you can see many 'Gangnam Dol': human-scale bear dolls representing famous, mostly second-generation K-Pop artists. Gangnam Dol derives from the words 'Gangnam' and 'doll'. There is even a dedicated 'Gangnam Dol' for BTS towards the end of the road (number 12 out of 17 dolls).

2 Days in Seoul

Day 1

9 am: Gyeongbokgung

11 am: Bukchon Hanok Village

1 pm: Museum date: HYBE Headquarters/National Museum of Korea

5 pm : Line Friends Flag Ship (see page 155)

The Line Friends Flagship store in Gang-nam, home of BT21 goods, consists of two floors. You will have lots of fun while browsing through the different products and you can also make memories by taking pictures with the different BT21 and other Line Friends character statues throughout the store.

7 pm: Welcome Home

One of the most interesting dinner places would be The House (see page 65). This cozy place invites you to spend a joyful evening with your loved ones over their specialty 'The BTS Tteokbokki' or another BTS meal set to share. This restaurant is a must-visit and definitely one of the highlights of this itinerary.

Day 2

10 am: Take some time for yourself in Seoul Forest (see page 102)

Seoul Forest is an idyllic place worth exploring because it gives you a break from the busy city life. Representing a variety of themes like culture, art, and experiential learning, Seoul Forest invites you to linger and take your time.

While taking a walk through the deepests part of the forest, make sure not to miss the benches dedicated to the BTS members. There are 19 benches in total and they are spread out, so trying to find them all will give you an indepth look of what Seoul Forest has to offer. If you come in the springtime, you will be rewarded with views of the famous cherry blossoms.

If you're tired of the hectic streets of the city, why not come here, relax and listen to BTS's music?

2pm: Exploring Seongsu-dong, the "Brooklyn of Seoul"

The trendy neighborhood Seongsu-dong is located east of the city center. It is not yet very popular among tourists, but it is a much frequented area by young Koreans who dubbed this area as the 'Brooklyn of Seoul' because of its industrial style buildings and hipster vibe. In the past, the streets of Seongsu-dong were lined with factories and only recently the old buildings were spiced up into cafés, bakeries, designer clothing stores and restaurants. Get lost in the alleys of Seongsu-dong and maybe you will spot some of the iconic street art the area is also renowned for.

4 pm: Coffee Break at Mellower (see page 105)

Seongsu-dong is paradise for coffee lovers with the number of cafés. Take a coffee break at the popular Mellower café. Well known among young Koreans, BTS member j-hope also once took a selfie in the mirror-door of the café and posted it on social media. Perfect to create your next ARMY Selca Day shot.

6 pm: Eat dinner like a K-Pop Rookie at Yoojung restaurant

8pm: Visit the tallest tower in Seoul: Seoul Sky Tower

Seoul Sky Tower, otherwise known as Lotte World Tower, is located right next to Lotte World in Jamsil. It holds an observatory on its top 7 floors and offers panoramic views of the Seoul skyline from 556 meters up and is especially beautiful at night. Enjoy the last few hours of the day staring out over the millions of lights to get an idea of just how breathtaking and big a city Seoul is.

4 Days in Seoul

Day 1

10 am: For the heart and for the S(e)oul: Namsan Tower and Namsan Mountain Park

2 pm: Myeongdong

4 pm: Leeum Art Museum (see page 113)

Leeum Art Museum and its exhibits blend classic Korean history with modern

art. The permanent exhibition hall and the outdoor area on the first floor are definitely worth a visit.

These exhibitions are free of charge but booking a ticket is necessary before visiting. You can also rent an audio guide for the visit.

7 pm: Nodeul Island sunset spotting

Nodeul Island is a charming little island in the middle of the Han River perfect for a break. It has become a popular place, especially on weekends, since it has recently been renovated. They installed a variety of facilities, such as a residential building, a multi-purpose hall, and various restaurants, cafés, bike stores, and pubs that sell beer and makgeolli. There is a bus stop right outside the door, so it is convenient to get there. You can visit the island by foot or by bike.

Nodeul Island is even prettier during sunset hours and offers a stunning night view. The skyline reflecting in the Han River makes this place the ideal spot to take a break from the city and relax.

9 pm: Welcome home at The House restaurant

Day 2

10 am: Time for adrenaline

Would your visit to Seoul be complete without conquering the so-called 'Disneyland of Korea' - Lotte World? (see page 80) Probably not. Any fan of K-Pop or K-Dramas would not want to miss it. If you're looking for a bit of adrenaline, the amusement park composed of indoor and outdoor areas is definitely a must-do for you. From electrifying roller coaster rides to more child-friendly attractions, Lotte World guarantees fun for everyone. Since there are often long waiting times for the rides, a visit to Lotte World can easily take up half of a day. Lunch and snack options are easily found in the amusement park.

If you are looking for a different type of activity which is also less time consuming, the Lotte World Tower and its Seoul Sky Tower, located right next to Lotte World, is a great alternative to the amusement park (see page 80). The observatory, occupying the last 7 floors of the 556 meter high skyscraper offers normal observation floors as well as glass skywalks, an outdoor terrace and coffee shops. They recently opened the 'Sky Bridge.' This could add a little more fun for the adrenaline junkies among you. Soak up the view of miniature Seoul beneath you from 556 meters above the ground.

Both attractions are located in the Jamsil area, a trendy, dynamic but underestimated neighborhood. The residential area often seems to be outshined by its neighbor Gangnam, but is gradually developing with interesting concept cafés, nondescript bars and boutiques.

Apart from the small businesses mentioned, a big part of the Lotte group's establishments are in this area. You can find duty-free shopping malls, as well as residential buildings in Jamsil.

1 pm: Time to sit back

Head over to Seiro Mushi (오쓰 세이로 무시) (see page 82), the restaurant owned by Jin's brother, to enjoy a tasty Japanese meal in a private and intimate atmosphere. The restaurant can be found amongst a variety of cozy cafés and

restaurants in Jamsil. Don't be tricked by the inconspicuous appearance of the restaurant - the taste of the food and the friendly staff makes you want to visit Seiro Mushi again and again.

3 pm: Where it all began

To fulfill the ultimate 'On the footsteps of BTS's you should head over to the place where their adventure began. Take a stroll through the alleys of Gangnam along the place where their first dormitory (see page 42) and the first BigHit Building (see page 45) were. This walk will make you realize how small they started and how big they have gotten now. The old buildings seem tiny compared to the huge HYBE building. It goes to show that hard work always pays off.

4 pm: Start feeling like your favorites

To make you feel closer to your favorite people, why don't you consider sharing the same piece of jewelry? Besides all of their expensive jewelry, our favorite 7 boys often wear jewelry from Frica (see page 54) or Hanna543 (see page 55) which is mostly very fashionable and affordable jewelry. Both stores are located very close to each other. Stop by and look around, you may find something you like.

6 pm: Time for some seafood

If you are a fan of sushi, you should definitely not miss out on eating at Eunhaeng-Gol (Gangnam branch - 은행골 강남역점) (see page 66). While enjoying high quality seafood, admire the 6 out of 7 signatures of the BTS members. This is the perfect food to finish off an adventurous day in Seoul.

Day 3

9 am : Gyeongbokgung

11 am: Daeo Bookstore café 대오서점 (see page 153)

Take a little detour to the Jongno area, where you can find the nondescript Daeo Bookstore café. Among a lot of other lovely little shops and cafés, you will manage to find Daeo Bookstore café in a small alley. The quaint café invites you to linger while you rummage through old books and pictures of movie scenes filmed in this very store.

2 pm: Yoon Dong-Ju Literary House (see page 150)

For the literature enthusiasts, make sure to stop by the Yoon Dong-Ju Literary house, a small museum about one of Namjoon's favorite writers.

3 pm: Afternoon hike

When you're in Seoul, you shouldn't miss out on the beautiful hiking trails in the middle of the city. Consider checking out the Inwangsan Jarak-gil trail (인왕산 자락길) next to Inwangsan mountain, close to Yoon Dong-Ju's hill (윤동주 언덕).

On your way you'll pass the Inwangsan Choso Book Café (인왕산 초소 책방 카페) that gives you a stunning view into Seoul's beautiful nature that makes you forget that you are in the middle of a city with millions of habitants. They sell different books about veganism, and pastries to enjoy with a nice view of N Seoul Tower.

The highlight on this trail will be the Hanok Library (청운문학도서관). The hanok style library is very unique and rare since there aren't many hanok buildings left in Korea. Again, by the looks of this place you definitely don't feel like you're in Seoul, it is incredible to think that you're not in the countryside but in the middle of Korea's capital city. Make sure to check out the photo spots with the little waterfall and the Seoshijeong pavilion (서시정).

5 pm: Donuimun Museum Village (see page 152)

Teleport yourself to the past while exploring the Donuimun Museum Village. Located in the center of Seoul, the museum village's main purpose is to protect the history of the Saemunan area. The Museum Village is a must see for ARMY since it was used as a set for Run BTS! episodes, but it's also a very fun way to catch up on some Korean history, too. It is your chance to experience Korea's traditional culture through their nostalgic looking facilities. It really makes you realize how much Korea has changed over the past 50 years.

7 pm: Strolling through Insadong and Ikseondong

To finish off this day full of history and nostalgia, do not miss out on the Insadong and Ikseondong area. Insadong is considered to be one of the most important neighborhoods in Korea when it comes to culture. Not only do you find a large number of art galleries in Insadong, but also little traditional shops and family run restaurants. Ikseondong, located right next to Insadong, is an area with renovated traditional Korean houses accommodating little shops, cafés, and restaurants. The area remains mostly unchanged since its construction about 100 years ago and invites visitors to do some window shopping, grab a bite to eat, and just get lost in the charming alleys.

Day 4

10 am: Museum date: HYBE Head-quarters/National Museum of Korea

1 pm: Lunch in Itaewon

Itaewon is a unique area where you can meet people of diverse cultures and discover a very unique food culture. Whether it is Mexican, Italian, Thai, burger places, halal food, there's no cuisine you can't find in Itaewon. If you want to take a break from Korean food and let your taste buds explore the variety of Western inspired food, Itaewon has lots to offer. Don't miss Itaewon Shopping Street where a variety of shops, unique cafés, and of course restaurants are lined up on the street. It is one of the most visited places by tourists.

Hyundai Card Music Library

While in the area you can visit the Hyundai Card Music Library which hosts a jaw-dropping collection of vinyls, CDs, music books and magazines. Their store, Vinyl and Plastic, is also the location of BTS's NPR Tiny Desk concert they recorded in 2020 and a great spot to add to your vinyl collection. The Understage area, designed for smaller concerts, was also where BTS did their Grammy Museum interview for "Dynamite's" release. Whether it is the architecture or the history contained inside, this is a beautiful place to spend your time.

3 pm: Take some time for yourself in Seoul Forest

6 pm: Dinner time at Yeolbong Kitchen Yongsan 열봉부엌 (see page 37)

The nondescript restaurant with its cozy atmosphere is where BTS filmed their 'Makgeolli Live' which gave us wholesome chatty BTS content. Finish off your day while enjoying the delicious pajun and their special BTS Makgeolli.

Gangnam street

Neighborhoods

Gangnam-gu

——

First dormitory

Hakdong Park

Big Hit building 1

Yoojung Restaurant

Second dormitory

Third dormitory, Cafe Hyuga

Big Hit building 2

Big Hit building 3 MDM Tower

Ichadol Gangnam Main Branch

The Isaac Flower

Deux Amis

Frica

Hanna543

Café Camptong

Wooga

Ilchi Art Hall

Bellevue Lounge Bar

Janbiwo

Josun Palace Hotel

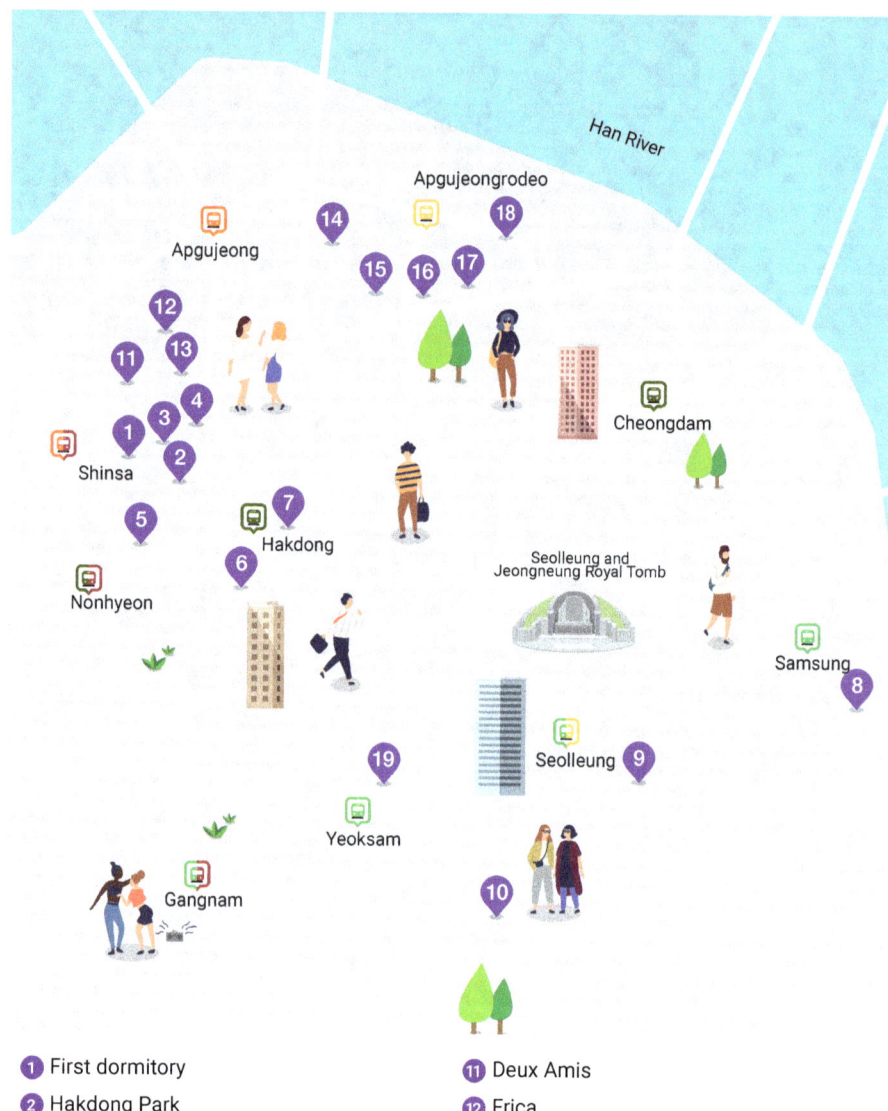

1 First dormitory
2 Hakdong Park
3 Big Hit building 1
4 Yoojung Restaurant
5 Second dormitory
6 Third dormitory, Cafe Hyuga
7 Big Hit building 2
8 Big Hit building 3 MDM Tower
9 Ichadol Gangnam Main Branch
10 The Isaac Flower

11 Deux Amis
12 Frica
13 Hanna543
14 Cafe Camptong
15 Wooga
16 Ilchi Art Hall
17 Bellevue Lounge Bar
18 BTS GangnamDol
19 Josun Palace Hotel

Gangnam-gu
강남구

Gangnam is a trendy, wealthy area often referred to as the 'Beverly Hills of South Korea.' A lot of you will perhaps be familiar with the name 'Gangnam' already because Korean rapper PSY went viral with his song "Gangnam Style" in 2012 and had the entire world dancing and singing along. The name Gangnam itself means 'South of the River' and the district is located in the southeast of Seoul. The song gained a lot of attention internationally with PSY making appearances in talk shows all over the world and performing the song for huge global audiences. The music video has gained billions of views on YouTube. It was the first time that K-Pop really turned into a cultural phenomenon. It was so impactful that a statue of the hands mimicking the choreography was set up outside the Starfield COEX Mall and a second statue by Gangnam Station. Despite its popularity, many people are often unaware that Gangnam refers to an area of Seoul. More specifically, it refers to the lifestyle associated with people in

Gangnam

Gangnam which defines itself by being trendy and giving off a certain high class vibe. You will understand what PSY meant once you walk down the streets and pass the first Shake Shack offering valet parking.

Some of the main attractions feature Starfield COEX Mall with its iconic library of floor to ceiling shelves of books, and the Galleria department store near Apgujeong Station, and some of the most prestigious restaurants and bars in Seoul.

First dormitory

"논현동 3층 고마웠어 - Nonhyeon 3rd floor, thank you" - Moving On

This is the place where it all started. The third floor of this building is the first dorm that they ever stayed in. The beginning of their song "Moving On" from their The Most Beautiful Moment in Life, Pt. 1 album is actually RM asking SUGA if he remembers how they used to fight all the time for no reason when they first moved together into this flat. The lyrics describe the place as being all blue, from the wallpapers to the bathroom and the veranda.

Located in Gangnam, near Sinsa Station, even the outside of the building makes you wonder how they managed to fit all the members into that one flat. Housing prices in Gangnam are quite high, which probably made it difficult to find an adequately sized flat for 7 people. Although RM says that he first felt like this place was big, he also mentions that

First dormitory

it was only 17 pyeong big (that's about 56 sqm or 605 sqft). If you listen closely, in the same line he mentions 9 trainees. You may wonder what he means by that: they stayed there in their early years, in a time where the number of group members was not set to the current 7 yet! Hard to imagine BTS as anything else but 7 members, isn't it?

They didn't have a lot of money, the place was originally an office that they renovated and used for housing. As RM mentions in the lyrics, as their ambitions grew, his own view on the flat changed: the house that used to seem so big now feels so small. He ends his verse saying that even though they lived there during some of their most difficult moments, filled with anxieties and fears about their future, and shed a lot of tears there, it was overall pretty beautiful and they should always remember it wherever they are. One of the remarkable things about the boys is the way they manage to accept both the good and bad parts of their journey as just what they are: events that had to happen in order for them to move forward and grow. In a way, looking at this building gives you a new perspective of what is meant by 'they started with nothing' and you can almost feel their burning passion and hunger for the world still lingering here.

Recently the members have expressed their fondness for the times they spent at their first dorm in their Run BTS! Special Episode Telepathy Part 1 and Part 2. In these episodes, as part of their second task, the members of BTS were separated into different cars and given codewords. For each codeword they had to think of a location in Seoul and travel there, but the aim was to try and read the other members' minds to go to the same place. For the first clue, 'real fun,' members RM, Jin, Jimin and V all decide to visit their first dorm. The remaining members SUGA, j-hope and Jung Kook also consider the first dorm as an option before settling on other destinations. In these episodes they also mention (and Jimin and RM visit) Hakdong Park, which is nearby and also significant to BTS as a place of contemplation, breathing room and where to make up over dumpling fuelled arguments.

The place is really close to where BigHit's first office was, it's only a brief walk to get there. You can really feel how far they have come if you compare this building to their 4th dorm in Hannam The Hills.

3F, 50, Nonhyeon-ro 149gil, Gangnam-gu
서울 강남구 논현로 149길 50 송아빌딩 3층
Sinsa Station 신사역, Exit 1 (line 3)

#History

Hakdong Park

Hakdong Park 학동공원

Minutes walk away from their first dorm lies a significant and often revisited piece of BTS history, Hakdong Park. This is the local park that the BTS members would visit during their trainee days when they needed to clear their heads. This is the site where Jimin and V reconciled after their notorious 'dumpling incident' and consequently where V began to write the song "4 o'clock." The vocal line held a performance here in their early days which features in Episode 7 of their first ever series Rookie King, in which they serenaded a small crowd of ARMY with their cover of Taeyang's "You're My." They also shared a number of photos in this park with various members, including on the steps of the pavilion, on some of the playground equipment (the one of Jimin wearing hanbok while riding a kid's seesaw comes to mind) and, perhaps most famously now, the swingset.

The Hakdong Park swingset is to the left of the pavilion if you enter from the street. There are two seats, and while they seem very basic and innocuous, many ARMYs flock here to get photos. The most recent reason is their Run BTS! Telepathy episode. After reuniting in front of their old dorm, RM and Jimin come to this park and sit on these swings to reminisce. RM sits on the green swing, and Jimin the red. They mention that the swings once had sand at the base and not the rubber ground coating it has now, as well as about how they used to practice the "N.O" choreography here. RM discloses that when frustrated he would come here, and while writing "No More Dream" and having his rap lyrics rejected 30 times he climbed to the highest point in the park to scream out of frustration. RM says, "This is where I took all my anger and frustration out." It's amazing to think that a little place like this contributed so much to the mega-band that is BTS today, but without that space to breathe and calm down, who knows what could have been.

The park and swingset seem to be important to all the members, even SUGA who came here for his 2023 Marie Claire photoshoot. He also chose the green-seated swing to pose on. The swings are of your everyday variety, so you absolutely can take photos and swing on them yourself for a little while. Just do not be surprised when other ARMY show up to take their turn there too.

You can find Hakdong Park between BTS's first dorm and the first BigHit building. From the first dorm it is a straight line to the park, walking away from the pharmacy at the dorm, and up the hill. The swingset and pavilion are right at the entrance to the park which itself is very calming to sit, enjoy a picnic, and walk around.

47, Gangnam-daero 140gil, Gangnam-gu
서울 강남구 강남대로 140길 47
Sinsa Station 신사역, Exit 1 (line 3, Sinbundang line)

BigHit building 1

As the years went by and BTS grew, so did their company. In a way, it is fun to look at and compare the different dormitories and office buildings that they have moved in and out of throughout the years because they become a sort of visual representation of their growth.

Although the company moved buildings a couple of times before they settled here, this is the place where BTS was made. It is near their first dorm, up a slight hill.

Big Hit building 1

(Perhaps you came here after visiting their first dorm and got to imagine what it must have felt like for them to walk up the small hill to work every day.) The area is rather quiet and a bit further away from the busy main street. Their office was on the second floor of this building. At the time, the company didn't have a lot of money to rent out a big office space yet. The difference between this building and the current HYBE building is so vast, it's almost difficult to wrap one's head around the idea of how big this small group and company have become over the years.

When you get here, you will easily recognize the building by its walls full of scribblings by ARMY who have visited the place. If you visit this place, please keep in mind that there are new businesses occupying this building now and refrain from adding any more messages to the walls.

13-20, Dosan-daero 16gil, Gangnam-gu
서울 강남구 도산대로 16길 13-20
Sinsa Station 신사역, Exit 1 (line 3, Sinbundang line)

#History

Yoojung Restaurant 유정식당

This is probably the most important restaurant in this book. Famously known as the place that BTS frequently visited in their trainee days, the restaurant has become a hot-spot for ARMY and a landmark in the history of BTS. In an episode of their variety show Rookie King, they came to eat at this place again. RM explained that they ate here often in trainee days, during school breaks up to twice a day, with V and Jimin saying they came three times a day. SUGA said he often missed his mother's food but the one made by this chef tasted just like home. The owner of the restaurant has expressed her love and support for the members on multiple occasions, saying they were not like the others and that she believed they would do well. If she knew how well they would do is up for speculation, but her trust in the boys was definitely not misplaced. You can

Yoojung Restaurant

Yoojung Restaurant

feel their impact on this small business, with all the walls and ceiling covered in posters and stickers of the members. Not only does this restaurant carry a precious part of the band's history and trainee days, it has now transformed into a small haven for ARMY.

Located in a small alley close to the busy streets of Gangnam, it is an easy walk from their first dormitory and less distance from the first company building. It lets you imagine what it must have felt like back in BTS's trainee days when they would enter the restaurant after a long day of practice and sit down to enjoy some delicious food.

· ·

Vegetarian options: Yes
Meat: Pork only

14, Dosan-daero 28gil, Nonhyeon-dang, Gangnam-gu 서울 강남구 도산대로 28길 14
Hakdong Station 학동역, Exit 7 (line 7)

#History

Second dormitory

Still in the same neighborhood, not very far away from their first dorm, is the second place BTS moved to. If you continue listening to "Moving On," you may wonder where the new 'higher' place is that they were moving to. Well, after moving out of the first dormitory they lived on the sixth floor of this building. Although they look back at the first dorm fondly, the lyrics also clearly express how happy they were to move into this new dormitory. The area is known as the 'furniture street'

Second dormitory

(가구거리) and if you walked here from the first dorm, you may have noticed a lot of furniture shops along your way. Unlike their previous accommodations, this was not an office beforehand. They didn't live here for very long and soon moved to the third dorm.

. . . .

Note: Keep in mind that this is a residential area and that there are other people living in this building now and be considerate. The last thing we want is to be a nuisance to current residents and reflect badly on BTS.

42, Gangnam-daero 132gil, Gangnam-gu
서울 강남구 강남대로 132길 42
Nonhyeon Station 논현역, Exit 10 (line 7, Sinbundang line)

#History

Third dormitory, now Cafe Hyuga 휴가

In 2016, when they were getting a lot of attention for their album Wings, BTS moved into their third dormitory. It is still located in the same neighborhood and not far away from BigHit's second office. Unlike the other buildings, this was a detached house. At the time, with their rise in popularity, more and more fans would find their way to the dormitories, so they probably chose this new accommodation for safety and privacy reasons. This is also the place they filmed the 'Blood, Sweat & Tears' VCR for their 2017 'BTS Festa Home Party.' After this, their housing situation improved drastically as they moved to the exclusive Hannam The Hill.

Third dormitory, Cafe Hyuga

In March 2022 this address became a cafe, Cafe Hyuga, allowing people, but especially ARMY, to see inside a BTS residence for the first time. To honor this, the cafe has left some of the dorm's old design, decorated with BTS art and photos of scenes filmed in each room. You can access and even eat in the rooms that members j-hope and Jimin shared, and SUGA and Jin. Jung Kook's room in the basement requires reservations to eat in, but you can still take a look through it. Only staff can access RM's room, but V's adjoining room is available and marked by fans with art and messages. There is a wall in the main cafe area (which used to be BTS's communal area, seen in Run BTS! Episode 29 where they become fashion designers for each other) that has hundreds of sticky notes written by

ARMY. You can add your own message onto the wall there too. The cafe offers the usual drink selections and baked goods, but the quality of their menu is worth noting as the cafe is popular with business people and everyday folk too.

16, Nonhyeon-ro 119gil, Gangnam-gu
서울 강남구 논현로 119길 16
Hakdong Station 학동역, Exit 4 (line 7)

#History

BigHit building 2

Nearby their previous building and BTS's second and third dormitories, in the area known as 'Furniture Street' (가구거리), is BigHit's second company location. They were using the fifth floor of this building. You can definitely see an improvement between the previous building and this one.

5, Hakdong-ro 30gil, Gangnam-gu
서울 강남구 학동로 30길 5
Hakdong Station 학동역, Exit 2, 3 (line 7)

#History

BigHit building 3 MDM Tower

This was the last office before they moved to the HYBE building in Yongsan

Big Hit building 2

in May 2021. They rented a space owned by MDM on the second and third floor. The security around this building is quite tight and it's difficult for outsiders to get in, so they did not have to worry about fans waiting outside to see the group.

42, Teheran-ro 108gil, Gangnam-gu
서울 강남구 테헤란로 108길 42
Samsung Station 삼성역, Exit 2, 3 (line 2)

#History

Ichadol Gangnam Main Branch 이차돌 강남

This restaurant, also referred to as 'Lee-chadol,' is where the BTS members reconvened at the end of their Run BTS! Telepathy special episodes. It is a BBQ restaurant chain that specializes in beef brisket. The members came to the Gangnam main branch to eat and film. This is also where Jung Kook casually suggested he would like to try "flying yoga," leading to their later special flying yoga episode of Run BTS! - they actually use this exact same clip as proof of where the idea came from.

There was a special purple menu created for the episode and the members ordered the 'Remember Side Set" which served savory brisket and short plate, doenjang jjigae(soy bean soup), jjolmyeon (cold

noodles) and chobap (sushi). You may even be able to see if the members left their signatures here while enjoying some delicious and world-famous KBBQ.

24, Seonreung-ro 86gil, Gangnam-gu
서울 강남구 선릉로 86길 24
Seonreung Station 선릉역, Exit 1, 2 (line 2,
Suin-Bundang line 수인분당)

#RunBTS

The Isaac Flower 더이삭플라워

The 99th episode of Run BTS! was set in this flower shop and featured the members learning about and working with flowers. The concept of this episode was a 'one day class,' a concept that is very popular in Korea. These classes give you a chance to try out different crafts for a day and maybe discover new hobbies. The most unique aspect about this place is probably its owner, Kim Isaac. The episode shows all 7 members becoming charmed by their teacher, so naturally ARMY has also gained interest in the handsome florist. He got really popular on TikTok under the handle 'Flowerboy Isaac,' sharing videos of his flower artwork but also simple videos of himself having fun.

The members really enjoyed learning about flowers and creating their own flower art. At the end of the episode, each member took their creations from the craft class home. This place is a must for everyone that loves plants and might need a coffee break. If you want to try a one day class too, you can make a reservation through Naver and have the experience yourself.

313, Eonju-ro, Gangnam-gu
서울 강남구 언주로 313
Hanti Station 한티역, Exit 7 (Suin-Bundang line 수인분당)

#RunBTS

Deux Amis 듀자미

In the same area as their first three dorms and Big Hit's first two buildings is this lovely cafe called Deux Amis (French for 'Two Friends'). It is best known for its delicious desserts. On September 9th 2017, Hitman Bang uploaded a selfie of him and j-hope at this café, where you can see a piece of dark chocolate cake, strawberry tiramisu and a green tea mille feuille on their table. The café stretches itself over two floors, the second floor being nice and bright thanks to the windows.

Café culture in Korea, especially Seoul, is quite special. As you will notice, the streets are full of coffee shops and you will meet a lot of people in the streets carrying their drinks around while running to and fro. There are all sorts of cafés in Korea: themed cafés, study cafés, coffee shops for a quick takeout, cafés with animals, the list goes on. Each place has its charm and atmosphere, so there is definitely something for everyone's taste. One of the most interesting aspects of this café culture is the desserts. You can find all sorts of delicious pastry in cafés. Whether you are craving cake, cookies, egg tarts, or bread, there is always a coffee shop offering at least two of these options just around the corner. In Korea, pastries are offered in various styles and many cafés usually give their own twist on their desserts. You can find croissants

Deux Amis

Deux Amis

with different toppings and fillings, macarons bigger than eggs, bread in many variations, egg tarts with fillings, there are no limits to the kinds of twists they give these dishes.

Besides the coffee and dessert, the cafés themselves are quite dynamic spaces. Whether you want to spend some precious time with your friends, have a business meeting, or prepare for your exam, you can always sit in a café. Most places have power sockets next to the tables and provide free wifi, which makes for a good place to work.

Students gather in cafés, since a lot of them either live in small studios with little study space or in shared houses together with a bunch of other people. So not only

are cafés in Seoul a good place to enjoy delicious beverages and desserts, but they're also dynamic social spaces.

While this specific café does not have that many comfortable seats for students or people who would like to get some work done on their laptops, it is still a cozy place to relax with friends or talk over some business. We can't be sure which of the two j-hope and Hitman Bang did, but judging from the food and their happy smiles in the photo, it can only have been a good day.

28, Dosan-daero 11gil, Gangnam-gu
서울 강남구 도산대로 11길 28
Sinsa Station 신사역, Exit 8 (line 3)

#SNS

Frica 프리카

*"I wanna big house, big cars & big rings" -
No More Dream*

This small store is best known for making handmade silver jewelry, one of the most iconic pieces of jewelry ever worn by any of the members. Frica made SUGA's four letter rings that he always wore on tour. On the store's iPad you can scroll through a gallery of images of BTS members wearing the items to choose from. If you are someone who can't decide easily and even less if there are many options, then consider planning extra time for this store because they have a lot to browse. Several of the members wore various pieces from here, with Jimin seemingly owning their entire stock.

The store itself is so small that if you visit with a group of five people, you may not even manage to fit everyone inside at the same time. The price for their accessory ranges from below $100 to above $500, depending on the item. In case you were planning on buying some earrings, it may be useful to know that they are not sold in pairs but individually. Their jewelry is simple yet sophisticated, which means it can easily be combined with every-day outfits.

This is a perfect shopping opportunity for all jewelry lovers and a perfect stop in between for those who merely want to have a look at the iconic SUGA rings.

Opening hours:
Weekdays: 12:00-21:00

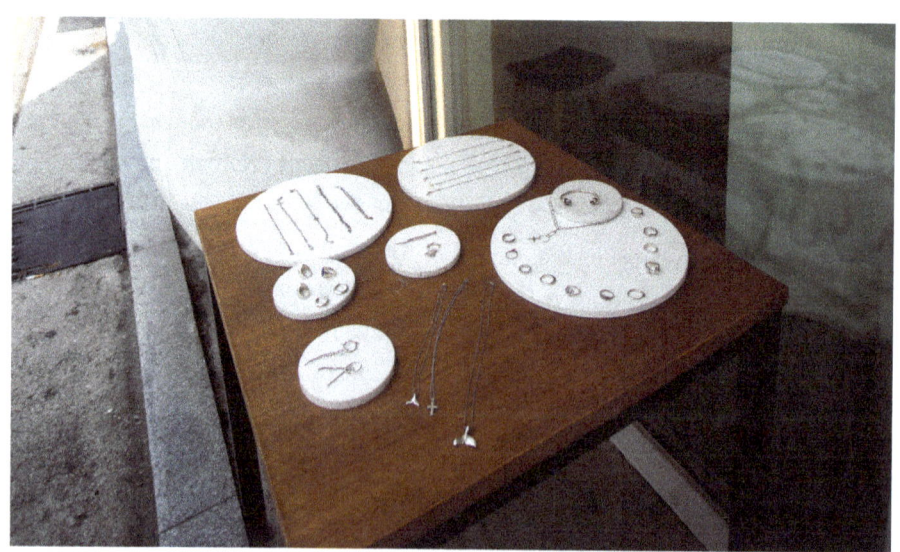

Frica

Saturday: 12:00-21:00
Closed on Sundays

49, Dosan-daero 15gil, Gangnam-gu
서울 강남구 도산대로 15길 49
Sinsa Station 신사역, Exit 8 (line 3)

#Shopping

Hanna543 한나쥬얼리

Hanna543

Another quaint store, located near the Frica store, is also well known for its jewelry often worn by BTS members, specifically Jimin who often wears their more delicate bracelets. Slightly less expensive than Frica, this store offers a different, more colorful style of jewelry. While they do not provide an iPad to look at what the members wore, you can either check their official Instagram account or ask the staff who will gladly show you the most popular items.

Opening hours:
Weekdays: 11:00 - 22:00
Saturday: 11:00 - 22:00
Sunday: 12:00 - 21:00
Monday: 12:00 - 22:00

49, Nonhyeon-ro 153gil, Gangnam-gu
서울 강남구 논현로 153길 49
Sinsa Station 신사역, Exit 8 (line 3)

#Shopping

Café Camptong 카페 캠프통

Another example of cafés as dynamic social spaces is Café Camptong. Stretching over four floors, this cafe offers a space to enjoy coffee and cake, space to study, several meeting and media rooms, a massage chair room, and other facilities such as showers and napping rooms. In the introduction on their official website, they said that they wanted to create an offline space for people to come together to create miracles (and various contents).

This location is a perfect fit for a Run BTS! episode with its size big enough to fit a film crew and 7 chaotic members. The café's aim to bring people and their inspiration together aligns BTS's philosophy about uniting people and

Café Camptong

reinventing music. They filmed episodes 118 and 119 of Run BTS! here. In those episodes, they had missions to take photos with specific instructions, such as poses, locations and who had to be in the photo. As one would expect, the episodes quickly fell into chaos as some members tried to fulfill their challenges and others resort to sabotage. The climax of the episode hits when the director reveals there is a spy among them, resulting in accusations, theories and overall entertainment for the viewers.

Although these things are now gone, the café had a purple wall on the first floor dedicated to BTS and ARMY, with balloons spelling out 'I Purple You.' There was also a section dedicated to RM's first mixtape RM. On the second floor,

there was an upside-down Christmas Tree with purple lights that had all the BT21 plushies sitting on it, and on the spot where the group sat for the final score and reveal of the spy, there was a huge projector that played the Run BTS! episodes onto the wall. Some of the photos the members took that day are still hanging up on the walls, for example, the selfie that Jimin, Jin, and SUGA took in front of the dart boards.

The café is also accessible by car and offers parking space.

27, Apgujeong-ro 42gil, Gangnam-gu
서울 강남구 압구정로 42길 27
Apgujeong Rodeo Station 압구정로데오역,
Exit 5, 6 (Suin-bundang line 수인분당)/
Apgujeong Station 압구정역, Exit 3 (line 3)

#RunBTS

Wooga 우가

Song suggestion: "Skit: Billboard Music Awards Speech" (Love Yourself: Her), "Dope" (The Most Beautiful Moment In Life, Pt.1)

Koreans' love for delicious food means that they don't mind standing in line for hours in front of a restaurant. One of the things they appreciate and enjoy the most is good, high quality meat. On the more expensive side, this restaurant whose slogan is meat science, is best known for its unique way of preparing local beef. A set of stairs leads down into a comfortable atmosphere and here they prepare the beef on the table with a blow torch, which makes every meal an interesting experience. For those of you who can't eat beef or generally don't eat meat, you can enjoy the vegetable bibimbap.

On September 30th, 2017, BTS kept their promise of doing an eating broadcast, known as a mukbang, if they won a Billboard award. They filmed this gift-like broadcast here at this restaurant, in one of its private rooms. Their oldest member Jin introduced Wooga to them, but unfortunately did not join them for this meal because he was home, sick with a cold. (They reassured fans that he was okay and even sent him a selfie of them eating to make sure he was not left out).

Earlier that year on May 21st, they won their first ever Billboard award for 'Top Social Artist' (a fan-voted award). Justin

Wooga

Bieber previously won this award for 6 consecutive years before BTS received it in 2017. They later included their acceptance speech as a skit on their Love Yourself: Her album. Though the award is now discontinued, BTS went on to win this award every year for a total of 5 times, nearly breaking Justin Bieber's record. In the same live, they spoke about not knowing what kind of vows to make if they were to make it to the Billboard Top 100 charts, which they would achieve three years later landing several number ones with "Dynamite," "Life Goes On," "Butter," "Permission to Dance" and their version of "Savage Love."

In a way, this place is quite meaningful because not only did they celebrate a new milestone in their career here, but it is also a place full of their future aspirations that would come true later. For many ARMY around at this time, this moment has become a fond memory. What better way to cherish that memory than over a delicious meal in a restaurant suggested by Jin?

22, Dosan-daero 49gil, Gangnam-gu
서울 강남구 도산대로 49길 22
Apgujeong Rodeo Station 압구정로데오역,
Exit 5 (Suin-bundang line 수인분당)

Ilchi Art Hall 일지아트홀

If you are planning to visit some of the other locations in Gangnam, you might pass by this seemingly random place. From the outside, it looks like any other building in the street, but it is an important spot in the history of BTS.

On June 12th, 2013, BTS had their debut showcase for Melon Showcase for which they performed their title track "No More Dream" and "We Are Bulletproof, Pt.2" in this venue. In a waiting room interview, they introduced themselves as a hip-hop group and explained that "We Are Bulletproof, Pt.2" is an extension of the same name song they made pre-debut in

Ilchi Art Hall

2010 to reflect their spirit. To the question of their goal for the future, they answered that in the short term they wanted to win the 'Best New Artist' award, which would be meaningful because only rookies can win it. Other than that, they wanted to become a group that people think of immediately when it comes to 'hip hop idol.' Little did they know that they would become arguably the biggest boy group in the world, exceeding all categories of Hip Hop or K-Pop.

Ilchi Art Hall reappeared in their 2021 Festa when the members reminisced over their early days and talked about their first showcase. V starts the discussion by remembering how they had to go out on stage one by one as the DJ was playing a song for them, with Jimin saying that the most embarrassing part was that they didn't get a lot of reaction. They giggle together over how nervous they were on that day, telling each other not to make eye contact backstage. j-hope remembered vividly how they performed and there had been no reaction from the crowd. SUGA adds that they first did the showcase for reporters. While discussing that day, the members agreed that most people that attended probably wouldn't have known who they were yet, with RM suggesting they may have seen them on a blog previously and Jung Kook agreeing that they might have just been

curious about the new boy group. SUGA too recounts that back in those days showcases were not as popular and most people would have just gone for fun. There were about 400 people who attended their debut showcase. They later also did some fansigns here for their The Most Beautiful Moment in Life: Young Forever promotions in 2016.

Looking at this building, it's almost impossible to imagine how they went from performing in such a small venue in the middle of Seoul to selling out massive stadiums all around the world.

806, Seolleung-ro, Gangnam-gu
서울 강남구 선릉로 806
Apgujeong Rodeo Station 압구정로데오역,
Exit 4 (Suin-bundang line 수인분당)

#Performance

Bellevue Lounge Bar 벨뷰

Song suggestion: 134340 (Love Yourself: Tear)

Up the street from Ilchi Art Hall is the lounge bar Bellevue. This was the set for Run BTS! episode 49, in which they celebrated the upcoming 50th episode by giving out awards for various categories related to past episodes, such as best MC, best cook, best sound effects, etc. In their usual playful manner, the members presented awards to each other while teasing the winning member at every chance they had.

The lounge bar has a welcoming and classy atmosphere, with an outdoor terrace. They offer a variety of cocktails and Western food, perfect for a relaxed night out with friends or a refreshing afternoon drink. It's on the pricier side, so it is the perfect place to feel the more luxurious high-end vibe of Gangnam.

30, Seolleung-ro 152gil, Gangnam-gu
서울 강남구 선릉로 152길 30
Apgujeong Rodeo Station 압구정로데오역, Exit 5 (Suin-bundang line 수인분당)

#RunBTS

Janbiwo 잔비워 (CLOSED)

This is a restaurant that Jung Kook and his friends had dinner at together. On July 28th, 2019, Jung Kook uploaded a photo of them to BTS's official twitter with the caption '구칠쓰' (97's). The '97 line refers to a group of friends from different groups that were all born in the same year and who sometimes meet up to have food together. In this particular photo, there are Jung Kook, Cha Eunwoo (Astro), Mingyu (Seventeen), and Yugyeom (Got7). Jung Kook and Yugyeom are said to share matching tattoos: an ox with the roman letters XCVII (1997) to represent their birth year, which was the year of the ox, and the word 'truth.'

Bellevue Lounge Bar

Age is very important in Korea and the first question you usually get asked from a Korean is 'how old are you?' That is because a lot of the social interactions are hierarchically structured by age, so knowing whether you are older, younger, or the same age lets the other person know how to address you. As a younger person, for example, you use different, more polite language to older people, pour their drinks and turn your head away when you are drinking alcohol with them. In return, older people often treat the younger ones and pay for their meals. You may have wondered why some younger BTS members call Jin 'Hyung' but Jin doesn't do the same for them. That is because 'Hyung' is a title of respect used by a younger man when talking to an older one. If you are the same age, it means you're both equal and nobody needs to behave or speak any differently: you can use casual language and don't have to worry about pouring your friend's drink all the time.

Though this restaurant has closed, it was important enough that we wanted to record it here for posterity's sake.

17, Dosan-daero 89gil, Gangnam-gu
서울 강남구 도산대로 89길 17
no subway

#SNS

Josun Palace Hotel 조선팰리스

This luxury hotel in Gangnam was the location for Run BTS! episodes 150 and 151, in which the boys tried a hotel staycation. Based on the outcome of a round of mini-games, each member was given a luxurious suite, with Jung Kook winning the first game and assigned to the biggest room, the Josun Masters Suite. After each member got their room, they started a video call with each other and the production team informed them of the real game. If they manage to spend and balance the unknown staycation budget to zero as a team, they'll win 7,000,000 KRW worth of gift cards. As they were ordering food and games to spend the budget, they correctly guessed it at 8,100,000 KRW and won the game by balancing it to zero on the dot with Jung Kook's iced coffee. The budget itself was a reference to August 1st when Run BTS! first started.

The hotel is conveniently located in Gangnam between Yeoksam station (역삼역) and Seolleung station (선릉역) on the green subway line number 2 and offers a spectacular city view.

231, Teheran-ro, Gangnam-gu
서울 강남구 테헤란로 231
Yeoksam Station 역삼역, Exit 8 (line 2)

Seoul Art Wave Center

Neighborhoods

Seocho-gu

——

The House

Jung Kook Forest No. 1

Eunhaeng-Gol Gangnam

Seoul Art Wave Center

Jimin Forest

Line Friends Store (BT21)

Han River

⑤ Jimin Forest

④ Seoul Art Wave Center

Sinsa

Cheongdam

Gangnamgu-office

Bongeunsa

Nonhyeon

Seolleung and
Jeongneung Royal Tomb

Samsung

Sinnonhyeon

Seolleung

③ ⑥ Eunhaeng-Gol Gangnam / Line Friends Store

Yeoksam

Gangnam

Hangnyeoul

② Jung Kook Forest No. 1

① The House

Yangjae

1 The House   4 Seoul Art Wave Center
2 Jung Kook Forest No. 1   5 Jimin Forest
3 Eunhaeng-Gol Gangnam   6 Line Friends Store (BT21)

Seocho-gu
서초구

Located right next to Gangnam, Seocho is part of the more general area that people refer to as Gangnam (along with the Songpa district) and is amongst the wealthiest neighborhoods in Seoul. Part of the district borders the Han River, where you can find the Banpo bridge with its rainbow waterfall fountain. The bridge is especially pretty by night so the area around the river here makes for the best late night walks.

The House 그집

For Festa in June 2018, BTS gathered here for their 'BTS Dinner.' Over some delicious food, beer, and soju they answered questions given by staff. Most of the questions required really honest, and often self reflective answers, so it feels like having a glass with your friends and getting all philosophical about life while still having fun. This may have inspired SUGA's show Suchwita.

The House is only open for dinner. At that hour, the restaurant looks pretty lit up with fairy lights that brighten the entrance. Inside little frames of photos from the 'BTS Dinner' decorate the walls.

Cute drawings of the boys gathered during Festa feature on the menu. They also offer a special 'BTS Tteokbokki' and a BTS set which includes three different dishes, perfect for sharing as a larger group. If you're looking for a place to get all emotional with your friends over some soju and beer, or even if you just crave some delicious food, this is a great place to spend some time.

46, Gangnamdaero 34gil, Seocho-gu
서울 서초구 강남대로 34길 46
Yangjae Station 양재역, Exit 8 (line 3, Shinbundang line 신분당)

#Festa

The House

Jung Kook Forest No. 1 정국숲1호

In 2016, in celebration of his 20th birthday, ARMY created the first forest for Jung Kook's birthday. Located in Yangjae Citizen's Forest is one of the most visited public parks in Seoul. The message on the signpost reflects the purpose of this forest: "to spread the fan's love & support for the star always and forever."

This location is not registered on official maps so you'll have to walk around a bit to find it. There's two different ways to get there. You can take the orange line number 3 to Hangnyeoul Station (학여울역) and exit through exit number 1. Then you walk down along the bridge (영동6교) towards the stream. Before you cross the bridge, there should be a staircase leading down to the park. The forest is right in that area. Alternatively, you can take the yellow Suin–Bundang Line (수인분당) to Daemosan Station (대모산입구역) and exit through exit number 2. Again walk down toward the stream. Once you're down at the stream, you can use the stone bridge to cross over to the side with the forest.

513-3, Daechi-dong, Gangnam-gu
서울 강남구 대치동 513-3
Hangnyeoul Station 학여울역, Exit 1 (line 3)/ Daemosan Station 대모산입구역, Exit 2 (Suin–Bundang Line 수인분당)

Eunhaeng-Gol Gangnam 은행골 강남역점

If you love sushi this is the perfect restaurant for you. BTS ate here and left their signatures on the walls. Looking at their signatures, you will notice there are only 6 out of 7 signatures. It seems like RM, who doesn't like seafood, was not with the rest of the band for this meal.

The restaurant is on the 3rd floor of the building and you can take the elevator up. From the elevator, the entrance to the restaurant should be right ahead of you. The restaurant is broad and the windows let in a lot of sunlight. There are also quite a lot of small tables, so larger groups of people may not be able to sit together easily.

Eunhaeng-Gol Gangnam

3F, 178, Seoun-ro, Seocho-gu
서울 서초구 서운로 178 3F
Gangnam Station 강남역, Exit 10 (line 2,
Shinbundang line 수인분당)

#DailyLife

Seoul Art Wave Center
서울웨이브아트센터

The Seoul Art Wave Center, a floating three-story building at the Jamwon Hangang Park, opened in January 2020 and has since become an important space for art and culture in Korea. The center has three exhibition halls and a Starbucks café.

On May 30th, 2021, BTS filmed their special performance video for "Butter"

here. The light, open space makes the perfect atmosphere for the fun and uplifting song. Not only is it a good space to enjoy art and a coffee, the big windows offer a panoramic view of Han River and the skyline. It makes for beautiful photos, especially during sunset.

A bit further down the road, still in Jamwon Hangang Park is both Jimin Forest (see page 68) and the spot where j-hope and Jung Kook ate ramen together one summer night in 2018. j-hope uploaded the video of him, Jung Kook, and his dog Micky onto the official BTS Twitter account. Han River is a really popular recreational space among Koreans and especially in summer you will find people sitting together on the

Seoul Art Wave Center

grass by the water having picnics, reading books and enjoying some leisurely time all throughout the day. There is always a convenience store around where you can buy and cook ramen, get some drinks and other necessities you might need on a day at the river. One of the most popular things to do here is order 치맥 (Chi-Maek) which means Chicken and Beer. Korean Fried Chicken is one of the most popular foods and it tastes all the better if you're enjoying it while watching the sunset over the Han River with a good cold beer in the company of your friends.

145-35, Jamwon-ro, Seocho-gu
서울 서초구 잠원동 149
Jamwon Station 잠원역, Exit 4 (line 3)

#Performance, #SNS

Jimin Forest 지민숲

In 2022, to celebrate Jimin's 27th birthday, the JM Sylvania Project raised funds to create a forest in the singer's name. The fundraiser successfully got enough money in less than two hours and this location in Jamwon Hangang Park was ultimately picked to host the project. In late September 2022, 800 fans joined The Seoul Environmental Association to plant 503 trees. 250 were Bridal Wreaths (Jimin's birth flower), 250 Heavenly Bamboo, and 3 White Poplar trees to represent the snow that Jimin loves. The JM Sylvania Project that helped orchestrate this forest said they hoped the Jimin forest would become, "a space to make happy memories with those who love Jimin."

Jimin Forest

Jimin Forest

To find the forest you can type Jimin Forest (지민숲) into your navigation app. Alternatively, it is a 10 minute walk from the Seoul Art Wave Center, heading right if you are facing the river.

The forest has two benches: one has a plaque that reads 'Nevermind' in the same font as Jimin's rib tattoo (that is actually SUGA's handwriting). The other has the quote: "How do you feel when you see

Jimin Forest

me growing up? You've seen me since I was 19." There is a sign that declares the spot Jimin Forest, the mission in creating this forest, and a QR code to learn more about the project plus messages from the donors. The location is perfect to sit and watch the Han River, including a view of N Seoul Tower on the opposite side of the river. In the spring time there are many wildflowers that surround the area, and a pagoda nearby that is overcome with beautiful purple wisteria. It's also a very popular spot for people to walk, cycle or exercise, so prepare to indulge in people-watching here as well.

147-1, Jamwon-dong, Seocho-gu
서울 서초구 잠원동 147-1
Jamwon Station 잠원역, Exit 4 (line 3) / Sinsa Station 신사역, Exit 5 (line 3, Sinbundang line)

Line Friends Store (BT21)

In 2017, BTS collaborated with Line Friends for the BT21 project, for which each of the members designed their own characters. Initially, there were eight characters, seven for the members and one for ARMY.

There is RM's sleepy koala Koya, Jin's polite alpaca RJ, SUGA's cookie Shooky who loves to prank others, j-hope's dancing horse Mang (who is now unmasked to be a purple squirrel), Jimin's kind puppy Chimmy, V's little alien Tata who is curious about the world, and Jung Kook's athletic bunny Kookie. They also created the space robot Van who protects BT21 for ARMY. These characters are really significant for ARMY because they make you feel more connected to the group and have become little tokens of identification for ARMY to recognize each other in the streets. They're also very popular at concerts to express support for their favorite members.

The project was so successful that they took it a step further with the creation of BT21 Universe in 2019, where they created elaborate backstories for their characters. If you are curious about the creation of the project, they uploaded the series to the official BT21 YouTube channel, so you can follow all the steps, from the member's first sketches in 2017 all the way to the creation of the character's family and friends in 2019.

There are a couple of stores selling BT21 merchandise scattered around Seoul. Here you can buy plushies, stationery, clothes, electric gadgets, and other goods with your favorite members' characters.

437, Gangnam-daero, Seocho-gu
서울 서초구 강남대로 437
Sinnonhyeon Station 신논현역, Exit 7 (line 9, Sinbundang line)
Gangnam Station 강남역, Exit 10 (line 2, Shinbundang line 수인분당)

#Shopping

Line Friends Store (BT21)

Olympic Park

Neighborhoods

Songpa-gu

—

Seoul Sky

RM Forest No. 1

Jung Kook Forest No. 3

Forest V No. 1

Lotte World Amusement Park

Seiro Mushi

Olympic Stadium Seoul

BTS Handprints

Jamsil Arena

Olympic Park

SK Olympic Handball Gymnasium

Olympic Gymnastics Arena

Olympic Weightlifting Gymnasium

Olympic Hall

Han River

Jamsillaru

Mongchontoseong

Jamsilsaenae

Jamsil

1. Seoul Sky
2. Olympic Stadium Seoul, BTS Handprints
3. RM Forest No. 1
4. Jung Kook Forest No. 3
5. Forest V No. 1
6. Lotte World Amusement Park
7. Seiro Mushi
8. Olympic Park

Songpa-gu
송파구

Songpa is a district in the southeastern part of Seoul near the river. If any of you have been to Seoul before to see a BTS concert, chances are you have been to this district. You can find both the Olympic Stadium and the Olympic Park here. Generally, this area is perfect for anyone that enjoys nature. The Olympic Park makes for a great afternoon stroll and the area around Seokchon Lake also offers a nice breath of nature. For those that enjoy riding bikes, you can go down to the river and cycle to your heart's desire. Other popular destinations in this district include Lotte World Amusement Park, for those who crave that sweet rush of adrenaline, and the Lotte World Tower, for those who crave that sweet feeling of satisfaction you get when you buy something new.

Seoul Sky 서울 스카이

Opening hours: Monday-Thursday (4 time slots), Friday-Sunday (7 time slots)
They may suspend operation depending on weather conditions

Available time slots: 13:00-14:00, 14:00-15:00, 15:00-16:00, 16:00-17:00, 17:00-18:00, 18:00-19:00, 19:00-20:00

Price: 120,000 KRW (Admission, Bridge Tour, 2 Photos)
132,000 KRW (Admission and Bridge Tour, 2 Photos and 1 drink at 123 Lounge)

For more detailed price listings and to book your tickets online, check out the official website:
https://seoulsky.lotteworld.com/en/facility/skyBridgeTour.do

For those seeking an adrenaline rush but are too scared of extreme activities like bungee jumping or the like, then the Sky Bridge experience may be worth a try. This was the penalty for SUGA and RM in Run BTS! episodes 152-153. For this episode, they had a chance to get rid of all their accumulated penalties from previous episodes and chose this activity as a penalty for the loser of the episode. The loser got to choose one other member to accompany him, in this case SUGA chose RM, who had been teasing him throughout the game.

Seoul Sky

The Seoul Tower Bridge is inside the Lotte Tower and consists of a 45 minute tour of the bridge on top of the tower. You can book tickets in advance or on the day itself, but booking them in advance is better because there are specific time slots and limited space. You should try to arrive at the ticket booth about 30 minutes prior to your appointment. From there, you take the elevator to the observatory deck. The ticket includes the observatory deck, so you're getting a two-for-one experience. After checking your appointment at the specific desk for the bridge, you will receive a red suit to get changed into and you can put your things into a locker. Don't worry about your phone, they will give you a little special phone case to strap around your safety harness so you can take it with you and take photos once you're on the bridge. To get to the bridge, you take the elevator up to a platform and then you need to climb up a solid flight of stairs - again no need to worry because you're secured throughout the entire experience. There will be a professional photographer taking your photos, which you can also buy later on. After that, you will have some free time to take your own photos and enjoy the view, followed by a couple of activities such as doing jumping jacks. At the end you descend the stairs and take the elevator back to the observation deck. You will get a certificate with your name to prove that you participated in the experience and then you can hang around the observatory deck for a bit if you want.

300, Olympic-ro, Songpa-gu
서울 송파구 올림픽로 300 롯데월드타워
Jamsil Station 잠실역, Exit 1, 2 (line 2)

#RunBTS

RM Forest No. 1 RM숲 1호

One special aspect of being an ARMY is the fandom itself. Known to make donations in the members' names for their birthdays, and become involved in a variety of charity projects all year round, ARMY are always trying to find creative ways to give back and change the world. That is why in an effort to celebrate RM's birthday in a meaningful way, fans planted a little forest by the Han River in 2019. Located in front of the clock tower at the Jamsil Hangang Park, the forest consists of 1250 bridal wreath spirea that bloom from April to May. RM loves nature and the river, so fans thought this project would be a great way to honor him and simultaneously do something good for the environment. When a fan uploaded a photo of it to the Weverse app, RM noticed the project and commented 'NAMU JOON' with tree emojis, happy faces and

RM Forest No. 1

heart emojis. (The Korean word for tree is 'namu' so in typical RM fashion, he made a word play between the word for 'tree' and his name Nam Joon).

Donations made from fans all over the world funded the creation of this forest and local fans volunteering on-site planted the trees on the day. Through a QR code on the wooden panel in front of the forest, you get access to more information about the project and the messages from donors and volunteers involved in the project.

To find this special project, you can search 'RM Sup No. 1' or 'RM숲1호' in your navigation app. The clock tower is within eye view of the main entrance to the park, and not a long walk from Jamsilsaenae Station (잠실새내역).

This is the perfect place to feel closer to nature, BTS and ARMY.

65, Hangaram-ro, Songpa-gu
서울 송파구 한가람로 65

RM Forest

Jamsil Saenae Station 잠실새내역, Exit 6, 7 (line 2)

#MadeByARMY

Jung Kook Forest No. 3 정국숲3호

A little further down the road from RM Forest No. 1 (RM숲1호), towards Jamsil Bridge (잠실대교) you will find the third forest created for Jung Kook. Registered on official maps, you can type in Jung Kook Forest No. 3 (정국숲3호) into your navigation app and it will lead you right to it. Alternatively, you can take the lines 2 or 8 to Jamsil Station (잠실역) and walk straight to the river from exit 6.

Organized by the same fans that arranged Jung Kook Forests No. 1, No. 2 and No. 4, Jung Kook Forest No. 3 in Hangang Park celebrates Jung Kook's 24th birthday in 2020. There are two benches with quotes and music lyrics engraved into metallic plaques that are worth taking photos of, while the benches themselves are in a quiet part of the park with a great view of the Han River and Jamsil Bridge.

Jamsil Station 잠실역, Exit 6 (line 2, 8)

#MadeByARMY

Forest V No. 1 태형숲1호

Not too far away from RM Forest No. 1 (RM숲1호) and Jung Kook Forest No. 3 (정국숲3호), you will find the first forest created for V: Forest V. Established in October of 2021 (in compliance with COVID-19 guidelines, much like other

Jung Kook Forest No. 3

Forest V No. 1

forests created during the pandemic) national and international ARMY helped fund this project. You can type in Taehyung Forest 1 (태형숲1호) in your navigation app, but know that this particular listing can be slightly off. The forest is directly next to Jamsil Bridge (잠실대교), and you have to cross under it if you are coming from RM Forest No. 1 and Jung Kook Forest No. 3.

If you want to simply enjoy the scenery around Han River, you could walk along the park and the river and visit all three of these forests as they're close to each other. Traveling in cities can be quite stressful, so this is the perfect option for a more relaxed day. You can unwind in

the greenery, maybe have a picnic in the park, ride a bike, or read a book, and still feel close to your favorite members.

1-1, Sincheon-dong, Songpa-gu
서울 송파구 신천동1-1
Jamsillaru Station 잠실나루역, Exit 4 (line 2)/ Jamsil Station 잠실역, Exit 7 (line 2, 8)

#MadeByARMY

Lotte World Amusement Park
롯데월드

One of the world's largest indoor amusement parks, Lotte World was the set for Run BTS! episode 51. The group was divided into three teams and given missions to solve while riding the three attractions. j-hope lying his head down on SUGA's shoulder during the first mission on the pirate boat, a scene made even funnier by the Run BTS! editing team who added the sound of a computer shutting down, has become a popular meme amongst ARMY. At the end of the episode, their grand prize (spoiler alert!) was a ramen cooker.

This place also holds a precious memory to the group personally. In the 2021 Festa 'ARMY Corner Store,' Jimin introduced an entrance ticket to Lotte World as his memorable item. Before they debuted, they came here together to enjoy themselves. They reminisce over that

day, recalling that they were all wearing black, and talking about how SUGA didn't get to take a photo with them because he felt sick and went home early (apparently they rode too many rides and he was dealing with a hangover). To Jimin, this is a really fun memory with his members that he wanted to share with ARMY.

The other members also clearly think of this time at Lotte World too, because it appears in Run BTS! Special Episode Telepathy Part 1 and Part 2. In these episodes, as part of their second task, the members of BTS get separated into different cars and given codewords. For each codeword they had to think of a location in Seoul and travel there, but

Lotte World Amusement Park

the aim was to try and read the other members' minds to go to the same place. For the first clue 'real fun' Jung Kook chooses to go to Lotte World. Though he is the only member to actually show up there, both RM and V have moments on camera where they think about Lotte World and mention it's one of the places they had the most fun as a team together.

The amusement park is in Seoul and easily reachable by subway line number 2. It is right next to Lotte World Tower, another popular destination for tourists because of its shopping and entertainment facilities and the Seoul Sky Observatory. Lotte World offers fun for people of all ages and with most of the amusement park being indoor, it is also enjoyable on rainy days. The indoor ice rink is iconic and open all year-round, but especially popular during the Christmas period for couples and friends. No matter when you go, it is sure to be an entertaining time.

Opening hours: Their opening hours are subject to change so check online before booking your tickets. 10 AM to 9PM are the standard operating hours.

Before buying a ticket, check some of the websites mentioned in the Things to Know (see page 14) as the websites are known to offer discounts or cheaper options.

Entrance fees
1 Day:
Adult: 56,000 KRW
Teenager: 50,000 KRW
Children: 46,000 KRW
Baby: 15,000 KRW

After 4 (To enter after 4PM):
Adult: 45,000 KRW
Teenager: 40,000 KRW
Children: 35,000 KRW
Baby: 15,000 KRW

240, Olympic-ro, Songpa-gu
서울 송파구 올림픽로 240
Jamsil Station 잠실역, Exit 3 (line 2)

#RunBTS

Osseu Seiromushi 오쓰세이로무시

It's a well known fact that Jin and SUGA are really good cooks. There is endless proof of their kitchen skills, be that in Run BTS!, Bon Voyage or In The Soop. But did you know that Jin's brother also has a talent for cooking? It seems to run in the family. If you want to have a taste of that skill, make sure to stop by Seiro Mushi. Jin's brother operates this restaurant and is near Lotte World and Lotte Tower, just across the bridge of Seokchon lake (석촌호수). It marks the corner of an alley and is easy to spot because the white walls with its brown wooden structure

Osseu Seiromushi

stand out from the surrounding gray buildings. The main door opens into a narrow corridor, past little private rooms, and into the main hall which is full of small individual booths all in wood. Dim lighting and the low ceiling give the place a cozy and relaxed atmosphere.

The restaurant's signature dish is Seiro Mushi, a Japanese method of steam cooking in a bamboo tray. Each tray contains an assortment of vegetables and meat. They also serve a variety of side dishes, other meat, and seafood. There is no need to worry about cooking time, as staff will check back and open the tray for you, a perfect location to enjoy delicious food and spend time with friends and family.

Reservations are recommended for dinner to guarantee a spot. Use Naver Maps to reserve to "Dine In" or "Pick Up."

Osseu Seiromushi

30, Baekjegobun-ro 45gil, Songpa-gu
서울 송파구 백제고분로 45길 30
Songpanaru 송파나루역, Exit 1 (line 9)

#DailyLife

Olympic Stadium Seoul
잠실종합운동장 올림픽주경기장

In recent years, BTS have been per-forming in stadiums all around the world, including Korea. The fact that they started at a venue with a capacity of less than 4,000 people and were handing out flyers to strangers in the streets of LA begging them to come watch their show, but are now able to sell out the Olympic Stadium in Seoul for multiple days in a row perfectly illustrates their growth and success. Amongst the acts that previously played this venue are artists like Michael Jackson, Metallica and Coldplay (with BTS members were in the audience). They had several experiences at this venue before their first solo concerts for the 'Love Yourself World Tour' in August 2018: in 2015 they were part of the 'Dream Concert' (a large K-Pop joint concert where multiple groups performed) and in 2017 they accompanied Seo Taiji on stage to perform some of his songs.

This stadium was also the location for their last concert before the COVID-19 pandemic started, holding the two final concerts for their BTS World Tour 'Love Yourself: Speak Yourself [The Final]' shows in October of 2019. They returned for a performance of "Life Goes On" without an audience during the 2020 AMAs. In June 2021, they held the 'Sowoozoo Muster' in this venue, which was also held without an in-person audience but streamed live globally.

This stadium showed up again in Run BTS! Special Episode: Part 1 and Part 2. As their second task, the members of BTS separate into different cars and receive codewords. They had to choose locations based on these codewords and predict where the other members would go. For the first clue 'real fun' j-hope drives to the Olympic Stadium because he believes that he and the members have the most fun when performing for ARMY. Later, when the final keyword was 'ARMY', 6 out of 7 members went to Olympic Stadium as a place where they hold many precious memories with ARMY.

Note: If you take a stroll by the Han River between Gangnam and Songpa, close to RM forest, it is likely that you will pass this stadium.

25, Olympic-ro, Songpa-gu
서울 송파구 올림픽로 25
Sports Complex Station, 종합운동장역, Exit 6, 7 (Line 2, 9)

Olympic Stadium Seoul

BTS Handprints

The stadium should not be your only reason to visit Olympic Stadium however. There are various installations around the area, many dedicated to sports and the 1998 Summer Olympics, but there is also a special 'Music Star Zone' that includes the handprints of the BTS members. You can press your hands into those left by each member to compare size or fantasize about what it might be like to hold hands with them. Interestingly, everyone used their right hand for the mold, except Jimin who used his left hand. Though each handprint plaque does not have the name of the member it belongs to, there is a visual guide on the wall to explain their arrangement. But it is probably more fun to guess whose handprint is who before confirming it.

To find the handprints you can go to Exit 6 of the Sports Complex Station (종합운동장역). From there head towards the main stadium that has the iconic Olympic rings out the front. At this point you should see signs on the path to the right for the 'Star Street.' You will need to walk past this to find the 'Music Star Zone' that has memorabilia for various music acts who have performed at the Olympic Stadium. On one of the walls you will find the section dedicated to BTS, who share it with Seo Taiji, one of their musical inspirations. There are other K-Pop artists handprints in the area as well, including IU and Shinwa.

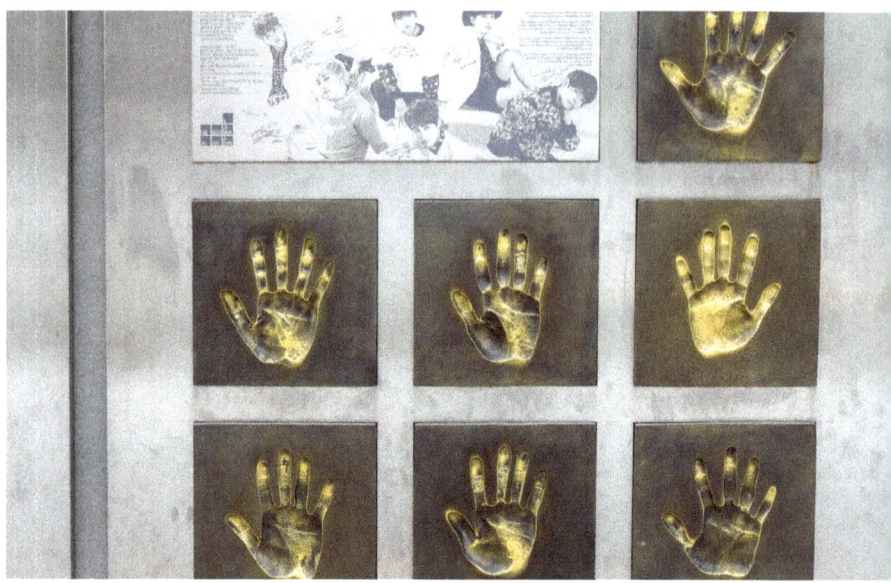

BTS Handprints

Note: If you go in winter or at a cooler time, be careful as the plaques are of a metal material and will be cold enough to hurt your exposed hands.

25, Olympic-ro, Songpa-gu
서울 송파구 올림픽로 25
Sports Complex Station, 종합운동장역, Exit 6, 7 (Line 2, 9)

Jamsil Arena (Jamsil Indoor Stadium)
잠실실내체육관

Next to the main Olympic Stadium is this smaller arena typically used for basketball matches. It is then somewhat fitting that SUGA/AGUST D, now a NBA

ambassador, chose this venue to host his 2023 D-Day concert as part of his solo debut. The venue holds over 11,000 people and every seat has a spectacular view.

SUGA's D-Day tour consisted of 25 concerts, kicked-off in New York on April 26th, 2023 then traveled to five U.S. cities. The rest of the tour moved to Southeast Asia and included Indonesia, Japan, Thailand and Singapore before ending in Seoul at the Jamsil Indoor Stadium on June 24th and 25th. The tickets sold out quickly, but thankfully the Seoul concerts streamed online for ARMY everywhere to share in the experience. On the last day of the tour, SUGA surprised ARMY by announcing an encore of 3 more concerts in August at the larger venue, KSPO Dome.

25, Olympic-ro, Songpa-gu
서울 송파구 올림픽로 25
Sports Complex Station, 종합운동장역, Exit 6, 7 (Line 2, 9)

Olympic Park 올림픽공원

This park was built to host the 1988 Olympics in Seoul. This event was a key moment in modern Korean history, as it was the first time the country opened up to the world and received major international exposure. It's an event that a lot of Koreans still remember. To give you an idea of how important it was, during their 2021 Sowoozoo performance Jin jokingly said that he still remembers the 1988 Olympics, to which the rest of the members responded with "you weren't even born yet." Jin stood by his statement and insisted that everyone remembers them, even if they weren't born at the time.

The park is now used as a leisure facility, where people come to unwind and relax. Divided into multiple zones, such as a cultural art park, an eco-park, and a sports park, you can explore the whole park for several hours. The old sports venues still hold events, amongst which were a lot of BTS concerts. If you decide to explore this park and want to try and visualize what it felt like to visit a BTS show here, keep an eye out for the following venues!

Olympic Park

SK Olympic Handball Gymnasium

424, Olympic-ro, Songpa-gu
서울 송파구 올림픽로 424
Olympic Park Station 올림픽공원역, Exit 3, 4 (lines 9 , 5) / Hanseong Baekje Station 한성백제역, Exit 2 (line 9) / Mongchon-toseong Station 몽촌토성역, Exit 1 (line 8)

SK Olympic Handball Gymnasium
SK 올림픽핸드볼경기장

This indoor sporting arena is located in the Olympic Park capacity of around 5,000 people. This was the venue for BTS's 화양연화 ('The Most Beautiful Moment in Life On Stage') shows in November of 2015.

Olympic Gymnastics Arena (KSPO Dome)

The Olympic Gymnastics Arena, or KSPO Dome, has a capacity of 15,000 and was the venue for BTS's 'The Most Beautiful Moment in Life On Stage: Epilogue' in May 2016 and their 5th Muster Fanmeeting 'Magic Shop' in June 2019.

Olympic Weightlifting Gymnasium
우리금융아트홀

The Olympic Weightlifting Gymnasium, or Woori Art Hall, was the venue for BTS's Festa Home Party on June 13th, 2017. They opened the show with a parody VCR of them recreating the 'Blood Sweat & Tears' music video in their third dormitory. Playing games and performing special stages, BTS showcased not only their talent as singers, rappers and dancers but also their fun personalities and humor.

Olympic Weightlifting Gymnasium

Olympic Hall 올림픽홀

This was the venue for BTS's very first fan meeting 'Muster' on March 29th, 2014. The following year, in March of 2015, they returned here for their 'BTS Live Trilogy: Episode 1 BTS Begins' shows in which they promoted their school series, including O!RUL8,2? and their second mini album, Skool Luv Affair.

Olympic Hall

Gwangjin-gu street

Neighborhoods

Gwangjin-gu

———

Andong Cham Jjimdak

Achasan Mountain

AX Korea (YES 24 Live Hall)

Achasan

Gwangaru

Konkuk Univ.

Han River

1 Andong Cham Jjimdak   3 AX Korea (YES 24 Live Hall)
2 Achasan Mountain

Gwangjin-gu
광진구

Gwangjin is a residential district north of the Han River and further to the eastern end of Seoul. Konkuk University and Sejong University are both in this district as well as Achasan, one of the most popular mountains in Seoul. Also located in this district is the Seoul Children's Grand Park, a park complex with a variety of facilities like an amusement park, zoo, and botanical garden. It features many attractions perfect for younger travelers.

The skyline around the Han River in this district is mostly made up of residential buildings and there is Ttukseom Hangang Park which offers a variety of amenities. Most of those are seasonal, so the park offers entertainment and enjoyment all year round. In summer, you can engage in fun water sports, and in winter you can go sledding here. In fall and spring, you can enjoy a variety of flowers and enjoy the beauty of nature.

Gwangjin-gu street

Gwangjin-gu street

Andong Cham Jjimdak

Andong Cham Jjimdak 안동참찜닭

This restaurant is near Konkuk University, the university that Jin attended while majoring in Film and Drama. Jin once ate at this place and gave them an autograph, which is proudly displayed on the wall. The place serves delicious jjimdak (steamed chicken with vegetables marinated in soy sauce) and you can ask for fried rice afterwards, which is served in a cute heart shape.

In his speech for "Dear Class Of 2020," Jin talks about his time at school and the most important lesson he took from it. He starts out by telling us that his memory of graduation is a little different. He said it was before he debuted as BTS, around the age of 20. He had just graduated high school, about to go into university, and he found the notion of becoming an adult quite scary. He shares how he was very cautious about everything he did and how he often saw his peers go on far ahead of him. While trying to keep up with them, he often felt out of breath and soon realized that their pace was not his own. He decided to make a promise to himself to 'take it slow' and eventually, that is what helped him through those times. His advice to anyone else who feels lost in the face of doubt or uncertainty, or the pressure of starting something new is to take it slow and not rush. Reminding us that every moment can become an opportunity, he wants us to take life one step at a time and take it easy. He ends the speech saying that we might discover important things that we were missing and they will reach out to us. This is quite meaningful if you think about the way he joined BTS: on his way to university one day, someone reached out to him as he was getting off the bus and asked him to audition because of his good looking face. Even after debut, he often spoke about needing more time to practice choreographies. As the eldest member to join the band, with no background in singing or dancing, he was often criticized in the early days for his performance. It seems that his experience at school and the promise of taking time for himself and not rushing to keep up with others still helps him today.

117, Dongil-ro 20gil, Gwangjin-gu
서울 광진구 동일로 20길 117
Konkuk Univ. Station 건대입구역, Exit 5
(line 2)

#DailyLife

Achasan Mountain 아차산

"We came as a punishment but it doesn't feel like one with this view."

At the end of Run BTS! episode 44, Jin, as a part of his penalty, cooks up a tteokguk (rice cake soup) for V and RM, who will climb Achasan Mountain and watch the

sunrise. V and RM received their punishments in the previous episodes 37 (RM) and 38 (V), both times from losing games and spinning the penalty wheel.

After arriving at the peak, V turns around to the camera saying, "Everyone, this is Seoul." (Here might be the perfect place to listen to RM's "Seoul" off of his second mixtape 'mono' as the view helps visualize the lyrics of the song). Sitting on the rocks of the mountain in front of Goguryeojeong Pavilion (고구려정), impressed by the amount of effort Jin put into their food, they express their gratitude for him and enjoy their tteokguk while watching the sunrise. Despite the biting cold, the two enjoyed the scenery

Achasan Mountain

Achasan Mountain

and V even concludes that although they came as a punishment, "it doesn't feel like one with this view."

This is the perfect spot for anyone that loves nature and sports, or anyone that wants to escape the busy city life for a while. The mountain is relatively safe and not too high, so it's great for beginners and less experienced hikers. The climb up to the pavilion is not too hard, so even those who need to take it easy can comfortably walk up and enjoy the rewarding view. It is also the perfect place to embrace the harmony of nature and big city life that makes Seoul so special.

Achasan Station 아차산역, Exit 1, 2 (line 5)

#RunBTS

AX Korea (YES 24 Live Hall)

This is the venue where BTS held their first concert 'The Red Bullet Tour' in 2014. The hall has a standing capacity of 2,500 and seating of 1,090 people. The three shows attracted a total of 5,000 people. SUGA refers to the AX Hall in his solo song "The Last" from his Agust D album where raps about the growth of BTS "from AX [Hall] to Gymnastics [Arena]," little knowing that he would have the biggest venues to brag about in the future.

20, Gucheonmyeon-ro, Gwangjin-gu
서울 광진구 구천면로 20
Gwangnaru Station 광나루역, Exit 2 (line 5)

#Concert

Seoul Forest

Neighborhoods

Seongdong-gu

—

Dongho bridge

Seoul Forest

Mellower

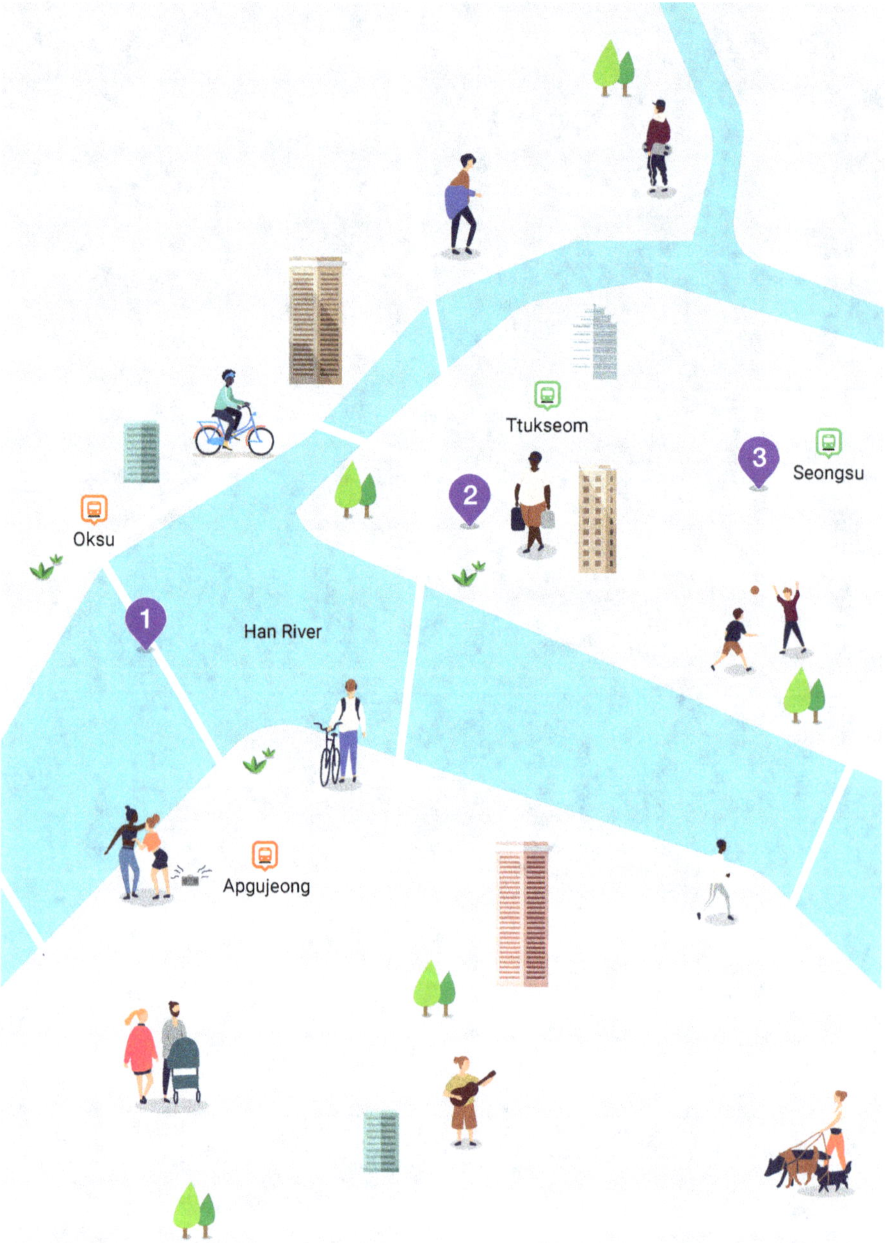
Ttukseom
Seongsu
3
Oksu
2
1
Han River
Apgujeong

1 Dongho bridge
2 Seoul Forest
3 Mellower

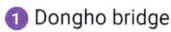

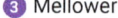

Seongdong-gu
성동구

Situated on the north of the Han River, in between Yongsan-gu and Jung-gu to the west and Gwangjin-gu on the east, is the neighborhood Seongdong-gu. Seongdong-gu is home to Seoul Forest, a lot of beautiful cafes, and has the Cheonggyecheon stream running through it.

Dongho bridge 동호대교

If you live and breathe for "I NEED U," you will probably recognize this bridge. This is the bridge where they shot the scene of j-hope fainting in the music video. As mentioned earlier, this song started the whole BTS Universe plot. (j-hope's alternate reality persona grew up in an orphanage and has Munchausen syndrome.)

'I NEED U' is very special for many reasons. First of all, it is the one that got them their first ever win at a music show. It was the turning point in their career when they really took off and laid the foundation for future years. It is also the beginning of the BTS Universe or 'BU.'

Dongho bridge

(For more information on that, check out the Dongjak Bridge on page 116)

But it's more than that, it also marks the shift of their artistry in general. BTS originally were mostly focusing on creating authentic hip hop oriented tracks, but something about the combination of the new sound, lyrics and visuals in "I NEED U" moved people in a different way. For many ARMY, this song was more than just music, it was a cultural reset. "I NEED U" was even chosen by Billboard in 2019 as one of the 'Songs That Defined The Decade'. This bridge now serves as a reminder for many ARMY of their first time encountering the BU and The Most Beautiful Moment In Life.

Oksu Station 옥수역, Exit 3 (line 3)

#MusicVideo

Seoul Forest 서울숲

Fan culture in Korea is a bit different from other parts of the world. Fanbases often gather a lot of money from donations to prepare all sorts of projects to support their favorite artists, such as ads in subway stations and bus stops, or cupholder events in cafés. Some of these projects are only temporary, like special installations or advertisements and specific events, but others are quite

permanent, like RM Forest No. 1 and No. 2 by the Han River and the benches in Seoul Forest.

Throughout the forest here, there are several benches dedicated to BTS members, typically part of such fan projects. Besides the benches with the little quotes from their songs, there is also a little garden installation to support V's self composed song "Winter Bear" which he released in August of 2019. Along with the song, V gave us a self directed music video, in which he travels through cities around the world. Since the release of this song, he is often called 'winter bear' as a cute nickname by ARMY.

The easiest way to find the Winter Bear Garden (nicknamed 'the Vench') is to use

Seoul Forest

Seoul Forest

exit 14 or 16 of Seoul Forest Station and go towards the Seoul Forest parking lot. In front of the Apple Tree Road you will see the lot for this V dedicated space.

Here in Seoul Forest you can enjoy the different types of trees and flowers while going on a treasure hunt to find all of the benches (at present there are 19 in total). Spread all throughout the forest, finding the benches should give you a full tour of the forest, and vice versa. Some of the easier benches to find are: the SUGA and Jimin benches located around the roller-skating rink. The SUGA bench inscription says, "Please lean on me from time to time and rest." The Jimin bench next to it has lyrics from his song "Promise" that says, "So that you don't get sick anymore, so that you can smile."

Two of RM's dedicated benches are also relatively easy to find. Head to the Ginkgo Forest and the path starting closest to the footbridge will have both RM benches first. These benches have the quotes, "Even as time goes on I'll be livin' in myself," from his first mixtape song "I Believe," as well as, "We are each other's nightscape. We are each other's moon," from his song "Moonchild" off his mono mixtape.

Besides the fan project benches, there is also the tunnel that SUGA shot his Love Yourself: Her poster at. It shows him sitting in the tunnel with the caption, "Don't come closer, you'll become unhappy." These posters were still connected to the BU, which is explained in the Dongjak Bridge section. The tunnel is in the Woodland Playground area and is the only tunnel in the area.

Seoul Forest is an artificial forest that opened in 2005 to offer a recreational space for Koreans. It is the third largest park in Seoul. You may consider it as the Korean equivalent of London's Hyde Park or New York's Central Park. It offers a nice opportunity to get away from the busy city and its high buildings to enjoy a green change of scenery. It is a great spot for picnics and has some playgrounds for the younger ones. It is a beautiful place to visit in every season, but is most well known for its cherry blossom tunnels in the Spring. Seoul Forest is also a much

beloved location for RM, who enjoys walking (and cycling) in nature. As part of their 2018 FESTA, BTS released videos titled "Sohwakhaeng (simple pleasure)" which listed things they liked to do. In RM's version his fifth item was 'going to Seoul Forest.' He says about the place, "I go [to Seoul Forest] and watch deer, and walk on the bridge that's located in the middle is something that I really like. When there are no people around...when I go there, I'm very happy."

While it is unlikely you'll have the forest without anyone around, Seoul Forest is definitely a must-see location while visiting Seoul.

Seoul Forest

273, Ttukseom-ro, Seongdong-gu
서울 성동구 뚝섬로 273
Seoul Forest Station 서울숲역, Exit 3 (line Suin-Bundang line 수인분당)

#Photoshoot

Mellower 멜로워

j-hope took a selfie in the mirror-door of this cafe and posted it to their official Twitter account. If you are one of the people who enjoy doing ARMY Selca Day photos, you could stop by here. It is a good stop if you want to experience Korean cafe culture more. The area is full of nice little cafes, all of which have a very unique atmosphere. This particular

Mellower

cafe is on the more hip side and makes for cool Instagram photos.

You will find a lot of people with a cool, casual style here. It's more of a cafe to relax than to work, although you can of course find yourself a higher table with power outlets in a more quiet corner. The cafe stretches itself over two floors and even has an outdoor terrace where you can enjoy a little view of the street and enjoy a refreshing drink in the good weather.

39, Seongsui-ro 7gil, Seongdong-gu
서울 성동구 성수이로7길 39
Seongsu Station 성수역, Exit 4 (line 2)

Mellower

#SNS

Hybe Insight

Neighborhoods

Yongsan-gu

———

Hannam The Hil

Hyundai Card Music Library

Leeum Samsung Museum of Art

National Museum of Korea

Dongjak bridge

HYBE Headquarters

Black Drum café

Superstar Tteokbokki

Yeolbong Kitchen

Haeswi The Wood

Silver Kit House

Blue Square Mastercard Hall

Jung Kook Forest No.4

RM Forest No.2

1 Current dormitory Hannam The Hill
2 Storage by Hyundai Card
3 Leeum Samsung Museum of Art
4 National Museum of Korea
5 Dongjak bridge
6 Hybe Insight, Black Drum cafe
7 Superstar Tteokbokki Sinyongsan
8 Yeolbong Kitchen Yongsan
9 Haeswi The Wood
10 Silver Kit House
11 Blue Square Mastercard Hall
12 Jungkook Forest 4
13 RM Forest 2

Yongsan-gu
용산구

Yongsan is a cosmopolitan district located North of the Han River in the heart of Seoul. It's a historically relevant district, as it was the center of economic activity for modern Korea. For many years, Yongsan was associated with the US Army base (Yongsan Garrison), which was once right behind the National Museum. Although it was relocated in 2018, the impact on its surroundings can still be felt today. Close by is Itaewon, Seoul's most foreigner friendly area, also known as the International District. It offers all kinds of international foods and stores that carry more than just the usual one-size-fits-all clothing items comon in most parts of Seoul. A bit further from Itaewon is also the elite neighborhood Hannam-dong, where many celebrities (including BTS) live. Overall, this area offers a variety of cultural and social activities to explore. You can either de-stress at the National Museum or have a drink at one of the trendy bars and clubs.

Yongsan-gu

Yongsan station

Yongsan-gu

Hannam The Hill

Fourth dormitory Hannam The Hill
한남더힐

BTS's fourth shared dormitory is a penthouse in Hannam The Hill, one of the 3 wealthiest areas in Korea. (SUGA even mentions the place in his song "Moonlight" on his second mixtape D-2). As you can see, they have come a long way from their first dormitory in Nonhyeon, to one of the most expensive areas of Korea. Security is really tight and outsiders can't get into the area, so they were able to enjoy their privacy here. It is also an ideal location as the new HYBE building is not far away in Yongsan.

In their 2022 FESTA dinner, the group got together in this dormitory to say goodbye to it. They shared that their lease on the place was about to run out and that, after living together for more than a decade, they each were ready to live on their own and thought it would be better for the group dynamic. In addition, they announced they were going to take time to focus more on solo projects in the hopes of growing and coming back together as a group even stronger in the future. Since then we have seen the release of some of these solo projects and which further broke the history records.

111, Dokseodang-ro, Yongsan-gu
서울 용산구 독서당로 111
Oksu Station 옥수역, Exit 5 (line 3)

#History

Hyundai Card Music Library

Hyundai Card Music Library

Hyundai Card Music Library
현대카드 뮤직 라이브러리

One part music library and another part music museum, the Hyundai Card Music Library is a multi-level archive of music and performance. The first floor is open to the public and consists of a lobby and cafe. The two basement floors contain recording studios and the concert hall, named Understage, where BTS filmed their online interview with the Grammy Museum for "Dynamite's" release. The second and third floors hold the famous collection of over 10,000 vinyls and 4,000 books and magazines on music, including 400 rare albums and a complete collection of Rolling Stone magazine starting from

1967. Here, Hyundai Card members can browse the books or choose vinyls to play in uniquely designed listening stations.

Next door and completely open to the public, is Hyundai Card's Storage, an art exhibition hall, and their music store Vinyl & Plastic. Over the art exhibition hall, is two floors, where music enthusiasts can find a curation of thousands of vinyls and CDs of their favorite international musicians. On September 21st, 2020, BTS held a NPR's Tiny Desk (Home) concert in this music store, which broke records for the highest number of live viewers at 600,000 and had 6 million views after 24 hours on Youtube. All dressed in a funky, colorful retro style and oversized sunglasses, they presented a variety of

Leeum Samsung Museum of Art

Leeum Samsung Museum of Art

stripped-down performances of their most famous songs accompanied by a live band. Those who may have wondered why they did not perform the songs with the choreographies will see that the space is quite small and perhaps wonder how they managed to fit the live band and all seven members in the first place.

. . . .

If you are looking to complete your album collection, it is worth stopping here.

248, Itaewon-ro, Yongsan-gu
서울 용산구 이태원로 248
Itaewon Station 이태원역, Exit 6 (line 6) /
Hangangjin Station 한강진역, Exit 3 (line 6)

#Performance, #Shopping

Leeum Samsung Museum of Art
리움미술관

Amongst the many museums that the members have visited is the Leeum Samsung Museum in Hannam-dong. On November 1st, 2021, j-hope and V shared a bunch of photos and videos of them having fun at the Leeum (M2) exhibition on their official Twitter. Later, on January 6th, 2022, RM also shared photos of the Leeum (M1) exhibition on his official Instagram account. In recent years, the BTS members' love for the arts has sparked a new wave of interest in these arts amongst fans, who started following their example. National news regularly reports fans engaging in "RM

Tours," noting the increase of visitors at museums after a member has visited. ARMY have even started using the term 'namjooning' to refer to activities that involve visiting museums, reading books, and just going out to enjoy and appreciate nature.

Located on top of a small hill in Hannam-dong, near Itaewon, the museum offers a variety of art exhibitions. Their two main exhibitions, M1 and M2, are free of charge and both stretch over a couple of floors. Both of these exhibitions compliment each other quite well, because you get to see ancient Korean art in M1 and contemporary art in M2, making it feel like you're traveling through time. It gives you the best of both worlds. They also have an exhibition hall for special exhibitions, which require separate admission. Be aware that even for the free M1 and M2 exhibitions, you need to make a reservation through their official website. (www.leeum.org)

Opening hours:
Tuesday-Sunday: 10:00 am ~ 6:00 pm
Closed every Monday, Seollal, and Chuseok

Admission: free

60-16, Itaewon-ro 55gil, Yongsan-gu
서울 용산구 이태원로 55길 60-16
Hangangjin Station 한강진역, Exit 3 (line 6)

National Museum of Korea
국립중앙박물관

On June 7th, 2020, BTS performed for the virtual graduation ceremony "Dear Class 2020." The event was for students of all levels who had graduation ceremonies canceled because of the COVID-19 pandemic, and featured speeches and performances from a variety of prominent people. They held the commencement speech inside the National Museum of Korea and later performed three songs outside by the steps. Both the event and the location are quite meaningful in the context of the pandemic because not only were the graduate ceremonies canceled, but the National Museum, a place that is usually filled with people, had to close its doors temporarily.

During the speech, each member shared their personal memories of graduation, hoping to offer comfort, hope and inspiration to all the graduates. For RM, it was his snowy middle school graduation, the photo of which he kept as his messenger photo for the rest of his school years. For Jung Kook, it was the self-reflection after rewatching his graduation video (available on Youtube), wondering if the boy in that video has really grown up to become the present Jung Kook. Jin shared how a promise he made to himself

National Museum of Korea

about taking it slow and going at his own pace has helped him through his school years, in which he often felt pressured to try and keep up with his peers' pace. SUGA opened up about how scary life felt to him at that moment and assured us not to worry, but instead focus on ourselves and the things we can control. Jimin expressed his concerns about everyone's physical and mental well-being while faced with the pandemic, encouraging everyone not to give up and to remember that in Korea, in the city of Seoul, there is someone who understands us. j-hope reminded us that we are the leaders of our lives and asked us to trust in ourselves, especially in difficult situations. V advised everyone to listen to their hearts when faced with difficult decisions.

If you want to see the exact spot where they held their speech, the museum has put up a poster on the wall next to it and seven stickers on the floor to indicate where they stood.

The museum itself is free of charge (except for special exhibitions) and is home to a big collection of history and culture. If you're planning to learn about Korea, this is the best place to visit.

Opening hours:
Monday, Tuesday, Thursday, Friday & Sunday : 10:00 am ~ 6:00 pm
Wednesday & Saturday : 10:00 am ~ 9:00 pm
Closed on January 1st, Seollal, and Chuseok (dates for these days change every year)

Admission: free

137, Seobinggo-ro, Yongsan-gu
서울 용산구 서빙고로 137
Icheon Station 이천역, Exit 2 (line 4, Gyeongui-Jungang line 경의중앙)

#Performance

Dongjak Bridge 동작대교

On this bridge, V shot his poster for the Love Yourself: Her album. It shows him squatting down next to a puddle and nostalgically staring at his reflection. It bears the caption, "If I had made a different choice, would they not have left?" Now to understand these posters in their context involves the BTS Universe. If you have joined the fandom in the years between 2015 and 2018, you will probably be familiar with it , and if you joined later, you may have witnessed your fellow ARMY analyzing comeback posters and trailers, wondering where they came up with all that information.

To put it in simple terms: starting with "I NEED U" in 2015, BTS created a fictional storyline called the Bangtan Universe

Dongjak bridge

(or BU). After the music video, the BU stretched itself through all types of content: there were the 'Highlight Reels' clips, in their physical albums you would get little notes with mysterious diary entries from the members, all set in the future, a Webtoon called "Save Me," two books and a mobile game. TBA is currently filming a drama based on the BU called 'Youth' set to air in the second half of 2023.

The storyline centers around the members in an alternate reality dealing with their respective anxieties and uncertainties. It concerns seven boys whose fates intertwine through the memories they made together. As they then go their separate ways, they all suffer greatly and one of the members of their friend group, Jin, gets stuck in a time loop trying to save them.

A complete map of this fictional storyline connecting all the BU related content was at the HYBE Insight museum. (See page 120) The BU was quite popular not only because it gave ARMY an active part in following the plot and making theories, always connecting the dots with every new release, but it also depicted relatable issues that fans experienced themselves. The way they depicted the reality of youth as something melancholically beautiful, filled with anxiety and bliss, resonated with the ARMY.

Seobinggo Station 서빙고역, Exit 2
(Gyeongui-Jungang line 경의중앙)

#Photoshoot

HYBE Headquarters

HYBE Headquarters 하이브

After BigHit rebranded from a music label to an entertainment lifestyle platform company, named "HYBE Corporation", they also switched buildings. They were previously using MDM Tower in Gangnam but now have relocated to Yongsan. The new building has a gym that the members frequently go to. It also seems that they have a company cat, as footage of a cute little cat has been appearing in videos and photos of all groups that are now under HYBE, with RM tweeting a video on June 2nd, 2021 of the cat jumping off his lap as a meme referring to V immediately deleting a tweet he had just uploaded.

The new building also provided a space for fans, called 'HYBE Insight.' It opened in May 2021, starting off with a special exhibition called "Seven Phases" by Taiwanese-American James Jean, held between May 14th, 2021 and November 14th, 2021. The first floor of the exhibition allocated music as experienced through its individual components of instrumentals, dance, and lyrics. Through different steps, the visitor could dive into the process of producing a song, learning about the various steps of recording, lyric writing and choreography. The second floor featured an exhibition of the Taiwanese-American artist, James Jean as well as interactive games to bring music closer to the visitor. The inaugural exhibition challenged almost all of the visitor's senses: seeing, hearing, touching and smelling. A curation of music into its components, from beat to vocal, lyrics and dance, all the way to fashion and appearance. The visitor learned viscerally what it takes to create music as an experience, emphasizing the art behind the music.

On September 28th, 2022, the special "2022 BTS Exhibition: Proof" exhibit took over the HYBE Insight to celebrate the Proof album and the Busan concert. This exhibition was to celebrate the past, present, and future of BTS through memorabilia and photographs. Inside, visitors could see iconic sets from their "Yet To Come" music video (and thus some of their older music videos), including the black-winged statue from "Blood, Sweat and Tears", the carousel from "Spring Day" and the red piano surrounded by flowers. There was another section dedicated to the photoshoots for every album and single BTS has done. Additionally, there were sections where you could find the members' signatures and messages written to ARMY. This Proof exhibition also occurred in Busan to coincide with the concert taking place there.

In January 2023, HYBE Insight closed its doors with promises of a new location.

The official HYBE Insight Twitter account tweeted: "We are closing our HYBE INSIGHT museum at HYBE's Yongsan building as of January 15, 2023. We appreciate your support and look forward to welcoming you back soon at a new location with more engaging exhibits. Stay tuned to our Twitter and website for all future updates. Thank you!"

On May 8th, 2023, HYBE Insight shared on Twitter that they were opening a new exhibit for HYBE label artists at a different location near COEX Mall in Gangnam. This exhibition focused on portraits of different groups, including BTS, under the collection name 'Daydream Believers.' Many people believe that this may be the new location of the HYBE Insight

Museum, but currently there has not been a confirmation.

42, Hangang-daero, Yongsan-gu
서울 용산구 한강대로 4
2Yongsan Station 용산역, Exit 1 (line 1, Gyeongui-Jungang line 경의중앙) / Sinyongsan Station 신용산역, Exit 2 (line 4)

#History

Black Drum cafe 블랙드럼 용산점

Though the HYBE Insight experience has moved, it doesn't make the HYBE building not worth visiting. It is a unique building to look at, and it's fun for the imagination to stand in front of it, take pictures with the various signs, and think about BTS working away in their studios. Many fans

Black Drum café

Black Drum cafe

especially enjoyed visiting the building on the night of j-hope's launch party for his solo album Jack in the Box, which took place on the top floor, and for that night was lit up in blues and pinks.

Another reason to visit the HYBE area is because of the cafés around it. Specifically, Black Drum café, located next to the back entrance of the building, away from the main street. This is a dedicated BTS-themed café for all 365 (or 366) days of the year. It's hard to miss, as it always has BTS posters and paraphernalia out the front, no matter the occasion. Once you walk inside, you have arrived in BTS nirvana as there are posters, cardboard cutouts, banners, balloons, merch, albums, figurines etc. everywhere. It looks small and narrow, but if you walk

through the room towards the main TV (surrounded by what is best called a BTS shrine), you will find that there are more seating areas around the corner too. The café is always playing HYBE artist's music, usually BTS music videos, live performances, fan cams, or sometimes documentaries. You can sometimes see other artists celebrated here too, such as TXT or Seventeen, especially around their birthdays or album launches. It is unquestionably a friendly and supportive space for any fan to bask in.

The food and drinks here are also extremely cute. Though on the pricier side, the drink bottles often come with stickers of the BTS members on them. If you're hungry then try ordering the toasties as they print the BT21

Superstar Tteokbokki Sinyongsan

characters onto both sides of the bread. You can choose the character yourself! The sandwich comes with a side of fries and some chewy candies as well. But the menu is diverse, so if you decide you want to get a bite, there will be something there for you. Also, the longer you stay at Black Drum, the more likely you are to strike up conversations with the owners, who speak decent English, or with fellow ARMY. There are many stories of people meeting here and forming long-lasting, genuine friendships.

11-21, Hangang-daero 10gil, Yongsan-gu
용산구 한강대로 10길 11-21
Yongsan Station 용산역, Exit 1 (line 1, Gyeongui-Jungang line 경의중앙) /
Sinyongsan Station 신용산역, Exit 2 (line 4)

Superstar Tteokbokki Sinyongsan
슈퍼스타떡볶이 신용산

If you are walking to or from the HYBE Building, and heading towards Yongsan train station (용산역), then you will probably pass the Superstar Tteokbokki restaurant. This is a restaurant that often has BTS decorations outside its storefront, especially around members' birthdays or new music launches. It is worth going inside because this store is also decorated on all four walls with BTS. You'll be able to find posters, stickers, drawings and other nods to BTS around the small restaurant. They also tend to play Run BTS! episodes on their TV screens and their music over the speakers. They do a lot of events and give away free merch (mainly posters) if you post about it on your social media accounts. Plus, it is a great place to try tteokbokki, a favorite dish for many Koreans, and one the members enjoy a lot.

In fact, in January 2022, an official report from a branch of the Korean government stated that sales for tteokbokki exports had risen by 35%. Much of that rise was because of BTS, specifically Jimin, who posted selfies of him eating street stall tteokbokki in Dongdaemun Market in 2019. This may have increased further with the release of Season 2 of In The Soop later in 2022, where all the members cook and enjoy tteokbokki together.

Tteokbokki is a dish made of chewy rice cakes (tteok) in a spicy red pepper paste, usually mixed with fish cakes (eomuk)

and sometimes eggs. You can buy it as a street snack, in which it is usually served on a skewer, or you can eat in a restaurant such as Superstar. In the latter, the staff bring a big pan to your table with the tteokbokki inside, and cook it in front of you. When you order here, you receive a long notepad in which you can pick what type of tteokbokki you want, how spicy you want it, and any add-ons you like (cheese is always a good idea unless you are lactose intolerant). It is affordable, filling and very delicious.

58, Hangang-daero, Yongsan-gu
서울 용산구 한강대로 58 1층
Yongsan Station 용산역, Exit 1 (line 1, Gyeongui-Jungang line 경의중앙) / Sinyongsan Station 신용산역, Exit 2 (line 4)

Yeolbong Kitchen

Yeolbong Kitchen Yongsan 열봉부엌

On July 25th, 2018, after a long day of practicing for their upcoming concerts, the boys gathered at this restaurant to have dinner and drink some makgeolli together. Makgeolli, a traditional Korean drink, is a slightly sparkling, milky, fermented rice wine. It's the oldest alcoholic beverage in Korea. Traditionally associated with the working class as a rural drink to refresh in between hard labor, it has recently experienced a surge of popularity amongst the younger generations.

During their dinner, BTS started a surprise V-Live for their fans, revealing that they were also working on a new album (Love Yourself: That album was answer which released a month later on August 24th, 2018).

However, the location made another appearance on September 13th, 2018, when they posted a video in which they revealed that it was a surprise Bon Voyage Season 3 destination reveal. The third season of Bon Voyage, which started airing five days later, took the boys to the small European island of Malta.

This rather small restaurant is in a less touristy area of Seoul and has an inviting, familiar atmosphere, perfect for intimate meetings with your friends. They also offer a special 'BTS Honey Makgeolli', which is sweeter than the traditional makgeolli, suitable for those of you who may not like strong alcohol but would still like to try this traditional drink.

46, Baekbumro 87gil, Yongsan-gu
서울 용산구 백범로87길 46
Namyeong Station 남영역, Exit 1 (line 1)/
Hyochang Park Station 효창공원앞역, Exit 2 (line 6)

#Vlive

Haeswi The Wood 해쉬더우드

In 2022 each of the BTS members put out solo vlogs, each with their own themes. Jung Kook went camping, V did a driving vlog, Jimin made metal bracelets, j-hope took us behind the scenes of his "Arson" music video and album making, Jin's was a cooking vlog with famous chef Lee Yeon-bok, RM took us on vacation to Switzerland and Paris, and SUGA's vlog had him trying a woodworking workshop. The workshop was this Haeswi The Wood. In the vlog he decides to make seven cutting boards, one for each of his members, and uses many of the machines under the guidance of his teacher. As he did a one day course, he got to try using a bandsaw, belt sander and did hand engraving. In fact, the piece of wood he practiced his engraving with is on display here along with the apron he wore that day.

In English this place is 'Hash the Wood' and doubles as a workshop and an online store. You can book your own classes, with options for one-day, one month or one quarter classes. You can make more than just cutting boards, including larger pieces of furniture. But if you would like to replicate SUGA's gifts then you can choose the whale-shaped cutting boards made from walnut and camphor and with a rounded edge.

Bookings are essential to visit Haeswi The Wood and classes are only available Monday-Friday 10:00-20:00. You can book using their website or through the Naver app.

38, Huam-ro, Yongsan-gu
서울용산구 후암로 38
Sookmyung Women's Univ. Station
숙대입구역, Exit 2 (line 4)

Silver Kit House 실버키트하우스

As previously mentioned, in the individual vlogs put out by the BTS members in 2022, Jimin chose to go to a workshop and make metal bracelets. It took less than 24 hours for ARMY to figure out that the workshop was Silver Kit House and to fill up all the bookings.

In the vlog Jimin makes two metal bracelets for himself. He uses (and breaks) two of the handsaws, files the metal and polishes it with plenty of concentration. In the vlog Jimin also writes his own captions and expresses how patient and kind the instructor was, something that ARMYs who have gone to this workshop reiterate as well. Jimin says his favorite part was hammering the bracelets to give them texture.

These types of bracelet making workshops are fairly common in Seoul and are inexpensive. Silver Kit House comes with the benefit of the friendly instructor and hearing his stories about Jimin though. Just make sure that you book in advance as the place is still very popular months after the release of the vlog.

In Jimin's own words: "If ARMY wants to try this kind of hobby too, or if you want to make something valuable for yourself in a quiet place, it'll be fun to go to a workshop like this."

6, Sinheung-ro 36gil, Yongsan-gu
서울 용산구 신흥로 36길 6
Sookmyung Women's Univ. Station
숙대입구역, Exit 3 (line 4)

Blue Square Mastercard Hall 블루스퀘어

The culture complex Blue Square Mastercard Hall has a musical theater, a concert hall, and two grand theaters. This was the venue for BTS's fanmeeting

Blue Square Mastercard Hall

'Happy BTS Day Party' on June 13th, 2016, and later for their 5th anniversary on June 13th, 2018 under the title of 'BTS Prom Party – Re;view & Pre;view.'

294, Itaewon-ro, Yongsan-gu
서울 용산구 이태원로 294
Hangangjin Station 한강진역, Exit 2 (line 6)

#fanmeeting

Jung Kook Forest No.4 정국숲4호

Over the years, ARMY have created multiple forests to celebrate Jung Kook's birthday (see page 170). In 2021, they created the fourth forest to celebrate his 25th birthday. It is along the Han River in Yongsan, quite near the HYBE building.

You can find this spot either by looking for Jung Kook Forest No. 4 (정국숲4호) on the map, or you can walk there from HYBE. Walk down the road towards the river on the right side of the street. The most scenic route is to cross to the Hangang Bridge (한강대교) and go down the stairs, walking with the river on your left side towards the train rail bridge ahead of you. Keep an eye out for this spot right after you pass beneath the train rail bridge!

312-1, Ichon-dong, Yongsan-gu
서울 용산구 이촌동 312-1
Yongsan Station 용산역, Exit 2 (line 1, Gyeongui-Jungang line 경의중앙) /
Sinyongsan Station 신용산역, Exit 2 (line 4)

#MadeByARMY

RM Forest No.2 RM숲2호

Given that the first RM Forest (see page 77) was a big success, ARMY decided to follow up the project with the creation of a second RM Forest located in a different area along the Han River, close to the new HYBE building and Jung Kook Forest 4 (see page 126). To celebrate his 26th birthday in 2020, park staff planted three hackberry trees and 200 spirea plants. Unfortunately for this forest, ARMY was not able to participate in planting the trees because of the COVID-19 pandemic and could only fund the project. The most special element for this forest is the little mailbox. Fans used to leave little gifts for other fans at the signpost of RM Forest, so for the second one they integrated a space specially made for these kinds of exchanges. The QR code on the mailbox shares a document where you can read birthday messages from ARMY to RM.

To find RM Forest No. 2 you can search for RM숲2호 in your navigation app. You can walk here from HYBE (see page 126 Jung Kook Forest 4), and it's less than a minute walk from Jung Kook Forest No. 4 (정국숲4호). Stick close to the river and you will find it. The mailbox will stand out, but also the two benches have plaques on them that are nice to read as well.

389-1 Ichon-dong, Yongsan-gu
서울 용산구 이촌동 389-1
Yongsan Station 용산역, Exit 2 (line 1, Gyeongui-Jungang line 경의중앙) / Sinyongsan Station 신용산역, Exit 2 (line 4)

#MadeByARMY

RM Forest No.2

Myeongdong

Neighborhoods

Jung-gu

———

Jung Kook Forest No. 2

Taoyuen – The Plaza Hotel

Star Avenue (Lotte Department Store)

Season's Greetings 2021

Jeonju Jib

Okagura

Alley

Billiard Hall

Café

Stores

Geumdwaeji Sikdang

Gyeongbokgung Palace

Jongmyo
Shrine

7

4 6

5

Jonggak

Euljiro4ga

2

3

City hall

Myeongdong
Cathedral

Hoehyeon

Myeongdong

Dongguk Univ.

8

Yaksu

1

Namsan Tower

1 Jung Kook Forest No. 2

2 Taoyuen – The Plaza Hotel

3 Star Avenue

4 Jeonju Jib, Okagura

5 Billiard Hall

6 Cafe

7 Stores

8 Geumdwaeji Sikdang

Jung-gu
중구

Located north of the Han River, Jung-gu district (as its name states 'center district') is in the heart of Seoul and the center of politics, economy, and culture. As one of Seoul's busiest areas, both by day and by night, it is also one of its oldest. Besides historically relevant places in this area, such as Deoksugung, Gwanghuimun, and Hwangudan, you can find some major tourist attractions here, such as Dongdaemun History & Culture Park. It's a suitable area both for people who are interested in history and for those who prefer the more modern cultural experience. For K-Pop fans this is the location of the Myeongdong shopping area, a haven for merch bargains. Besides the old Line Friends store that once sold BT21 characters, there are several Mediheal stores selling the BTS face mask kits. You can also find many little music stores that sell K-Pop albums as well as summer/winter packages and DVDs. This guide won't list specific stores because of the sheer number in the area and how easy they are to stumble across.

Jung-gu

Jung-gu

Tip: One strongly recommended music store is on the second floor of Nature Republic by Exit 6. Make sure to check that one out!

Jung Kook Forest No. 2 정국숲2호

One year after the creation of the first forest, fans created Jung Kook Forest No. 2 to celebrate his 21st birthday. The 'forest' is located in an elevated skypark near Seoul Station (서울역), called Seoullo 7017 (서울로 7017). The tree is in Magnolia Square but there is nothing to indicate that this specific tree relates to BTS. It is a lovely project to explore however, and some of you might be passing through

Seoul Station on your way to other cities, like Busan or Gangneung. So while you're around, why not stroll through the park before catching the train to your next big adventure?

33, Toegye-ro, Jung-gu 서울 중구 퇴계로 33
Seoul Station 서울역, Exit 7, 8 (line 1, 4)

#MadeByArmy

Taoyuen – The Plaza Hotel
도원 - 더플라자

This is the restaurant BTS ate for lunch at the end of Run BTS! episode 130. In Run BTS! episode 124, the members took on the task to decide on a theme for a long-term and a short-term episode. After some discussion, they agreed that they would like to try and properly learn tennis. As for the short-term one, they decided on 'Lucky Seven' where they would have to finish a series of mini games (episode 126). The tennis project stretched itself over two episodes (129-130) and featured images of the members on the field, but also in the training hall that they visited in their free time. With their single "Dynamite" ranking number 1 on the Billboard Top 100, their schedules got busier and they didn't have a lot of time left to practice tennis. In the meantime, SUGA also had to get surgery for his shoulder injury and worked as the MC for episode 130.

At the end of episode 130, Jin treated his fellow members to a meal at the Chinese restaurant Taoyuen after being crowned tennis champion. In their 2021 Festa 'ARMY Corner Store' when they were introducing memorable items, Jin brought the medal he won in this episode, saying that he had played tennis a lot recently and that he was grateful for ARMY to have given him a good hobby with good memories.

This hotel is also the set for Run BTS! episodes 131 and 132, which took place at the indoor pool. This is one of ARMY's favorite episodes because it contains many of the member's chaotic jokes. The theme of this pool episode was a

Taoyuen – The Plaza Hotel

77 minute debate session, where they would be given trivial topics to debate (for example, crunchy cereal vs soft cereal). Of course their discussions in themselves were already funny, but the staff added forbidden words and actions into the debate. For every forbidden word or action, the members would be sprayed with water and a huge bucket of water dumped onto the member moderating the current debate. The episode quickly turned into a watershow, with the members sometimes setting off the water punishment on purpose, and other times desperately trying to figure out the forbidden action in order to stop the water attacks. The pool itself is on the 18th floor of this hotel and is part of the hotel's membership-based fitness club.

Offering some of the best Chinese food in Seoul, this restaurant is a bit more on the expensive side. The atmosphere is very classy, and they offer private rooms like the one where BTS had their meal. Be sure to make a reservation in advance as the place is also a popular spot for business meetings and lunch breaks and can get crowded.

3F, 119, Sogong-ro, Jung-gu
서울 중구 소공로 119 더 플라자호텔 3F
City Hall Station 시청역, Exit 6 (line 2, 6)

#RunBTS

Star Avenue (Lotte Department Store) 롯데 스타에비뉴

Walking through the "digital media tunnel" in Star Avenue will let you dive deep into the K-Pop universe. It used to include the handprints of BTS members that, by touching these handprints, would have a coordinating member appear on the screen in front of you. Now, this Star Avenue does not feature any HYBE artists. But there are still some K-Pop screens to see and a store to buy albums and other merchandise. To find the BTS handprints, refer to our dedicated section in Jamsil [see page 86].

81, Namdaemun-ro, Jung-gu
서울 중구 남대문로 81
Euljiro 1(il)-ga Station 을지로입구역, Exit 7, 8 (line 2)

Season's Greetings 2021

For this next section, locations were divided differently because they are all part of the Season's Greetings 2021 and best grouped under that title.

The general area is located along the recreational space of Cheonggyecheon stream in downtown Seoul. The stream is also mentioned in RM's "Seoul" when he says, "I love the fishy smell of Cheonggyecheon," and is easily accessible

Star Avenue (Lotte Department Store)

for you to experience these lyrics for yourself. Cheonggyecheon was originally a stream, then turned into an elevated highway and was then restored into a stream again in 2005. It has since become a popular pedestrian space.

The locations chosen for Season's Greetings stand in stark contrast with the usual modernity that you would experience as a tourist on your regular visit to Seoul. The small, inconspicuous alleyways stuffed with shops selling less conventional objects are reminiscent of a different Seoul, before big franchises and modern architecture took over.

Especially in the context of the pandemic, where the future suddenly became even scarier than it was, it seems like a natural instinct almost to return to a familiar past. They released this retro styled Season's Greetings in December 2020, following the release of their Billboard Top 100 number one song "Dynamite" in August of the same year. It perfectly captures the nostalgic vibe that is also representative of the song.

All of the individual locations are easy to reach by subway and lie within a short walk from each other.

Because this area is so different from the regular tourist hot spots, it might give you a feeling of having randomly lost your way and ending up in a part of the city that does not even seem like it belongs anymore. Although it's technically not far away from modern Seoul, you might feel like you have wandered off into a different time and city, which makes the vibe all the more special. Almost like a little time travel in the middle of your trip, you can pretend that you are in the time that the sound of "Dynamite" was trying to mimic.

Jeonju Jib 전주집

This is the restaurant that Jimin stood in front of for his photos, the one where he wears a tracksuit and headscarf, casually throwing a bag over his shoulder. The restaurant has two floors of seats available and has a very familiar feeling, almost like coming home to your grandparents' place. They mainly serve traditional Korean food like kimchi jjigae (kimchi stew) and samgyeobsal (grilled pork belly). For those who can't eat pork they also offer other options like duck meat and tuna fried rice.

18-8, Chungmu-ro 11gil, Jung-gu
서울 중구 충무로 11길 18-8
Euljiro 3 ga Station 을지로3가역, Exit 4
(line2, 3)

#Photoshoot

Jeonju Jib

Okagura

Okagura 오카구라

When facing the restaurant that Jimin stood in front of and turn around, you will see the restaurant photospot for Jin. Wearing sunglasses and a neck scarf, he is casually leaning his arm on the window with their menu. The restaurant is quite small but the big windows that stretch over the entire front open the space up. They serve delicious Japanese food, including ramen and sashimi.

26-5, Eulji-ro 11gil, Jung-gu
서울 중구 을지로 11길 26-5
Euljiro 3 ga Station 을지로3가역, Exit 4
(line2, 3)

Alley

Still standing facing down the street, away from the restaurant that Jimin stood at, you might recognize the street as the one that Jung Kook stood in for his photos. With a gray animal print shirt sticking out of his sleek black suit, hands in his pocket, he is giving us lots of cool attitude. For his photo, the green door of the restaurant at the corner is open, so if you plan on retaking the exact same picture you should prepare to compromise in case they choose to keep it closed that day as well.

Another part of the alley that you might recognize is the electric box right next to the restaurant with the green door. That's

Billiard Hall

the spot where j-hope was posing with his red shirt and flashy yellow/green hat, demonstrating once again that this old-

Billiard Hall

school flashy street style was practically made for him.

Other spots include the colorful wall on the left when facing the Jeonju Jib, where Jin was leaning on with wide spread arms, and the garage on the opposite side of that wall where Jimin was standing playfully pointing finger guns.

#Photoshoot

Billiard Hall 우리당구장

If you are one of those people who enjoy a game of billiards with their friends, then you should check out this billiard hall where BTS took some of their Season's Greetings photos. It is located in the same area as the other photoshoot spots, up on the second floor. It looks inconspicuous from the outside but once you enter the building it's hard to miss.

53-1, Chungmu-ro, Jung-gu
서울 중구 충무로 53-1
Euljiro 3 ga Station 을지로3가역, Exit 9
(line2, 3)

#Photoshoot

Cafe 을지다방 (GONE)

Just like the alley in which SUGA, RM, and V took their Season's Greetings photos, this cafe no longer exists. It was on the main road, close to the other alley in which the members Jin, j-hope, Jimin and Jung Kook took their photos. Exploring this area can provide a general idea of the photoshoot, the differences or similarities of each location and adds to the general vibe of the Season's Greetings for 2021. An area worth the visit.

72-1, Chungmu-ro, Jung-gu
서울 중구 충무로 72-1
Euljiro 3 ga Station 을지로3가역, Exit 5
(line2, 3)

#Photoshoot

Stores, 제일귀금속/대원카메라 (GONE)

You may be curious about the locations for the other three members, SUGA, RM,

and V, these spots were only a short walk away across Cheonggyecheon from the alley with the other members. However, these photospots have now closed or changed to be unrecognizable. You can still take a walk around the area to get an idea of the kind of vibe it used to give, but you won't be able to visit the exact photo spots anymore.

30, Changgyeonggung-ro 13gil, Jongno-gu 서울 종로구 창경궁로 13길 30
Euljiro 4 ga Station 을지로3가역, Exit 4
(line2, 5)

#Photoshoot

Geumdwaeji Sikdang 금돼지식당

Geumdwaeji Sikdang

Geumdwaeji Sikdang

If you haven't had the chance to try the infamous samgyeobsal (grilled pork belly) yet then you should definitely stop by here. The name of this restaurant translates to 'Golden Pig Restaurant' and it has been awarded with several Michelin awards. It's said to be one of BTS's golden maknae Jung Kook's favorite places, but apparently all the members have eaten here before. At the entrance, there are even some BTS stickers plastered on the wall. The place stretches over three floors, with a regular 'original' eating space on the first floor, a bar space on the second floor, and a terrace-like area on the third one.

If you have never had Korean BBQ before, this is how you eat it: you grill your meat and then you take a lettuce leaf and place the meat in the leaf. Then you can add sauce, kimchi, garlic, or any toppings you like. You wrap the leaf and then pop it into your mouth in one bite. The coolness and crunchiness of the lettuce with the warm, soft meat inside, and the various other ingredients you add to your wrap will make your taste buds tingle for sure.

Unfortunately, this is not an option for anyone who cannot eat pork because their menu doesn't offer any alternatives.

149, Dasan-ro, Jung-gu
서울 중구 다산로 149
Yaksu Station 약수역, Exit 2 (lines 3, 6)

#DailyLife

Gyeongbokgung

Neighborhoods

Jongno-gu

Gyeongbokgung

Woonkyung Gotaek

Yoon Dong-Ju Literary House

Daeo Bookstore/Café

Donuimun Museum Village

Line Friends (BT21)

Gyeongbokgung Palace

Gyeongbokgung

Anguk

Gwanghwamun

Jonggak

Gyeonghuigung Palace

1 Gyeongbokgung
2 Woonkyung Gotaek
3 Yoon Dong-Ju Literary House

4 Daeo Bookstore/Café
5 Donuimun Museum Village

Jongno-gu
종로구

Home to most of the palaces in Seoul, Jongno is a district rich in history. About 600 years ago, the Joseon dynasty established the capital city here and it has since been one the most important districts both culturally and administratively. Here you can find some of the most beautiful palaces in Jongno, and there are parts of this area where you can still see hanoks (traditional Korean houses). In fact, the majority of cultural heritage sites that are official historical monuments exist throughout this district. That makes this area of Seoul the focus for most regular tourists. Among the most popular stops here are the palace compounds, the Ikseondong Hanok Village, with its small narrow alleys filled with cafes, restaurants and unique little stores, and Insadong the arts and crafts area where you can buy all kinds of traditional goods that make for nice souvenirs.

Jongno street

Gyeongbokgung 경복궁

Opening hours:
January to February: 9:00-17:00
(last entry 16:00)
March to May: 9:00-18:00
(last entry 17:00)
June to August: 9:00-18:30
(last entry 17:30)
September to October: 9:00-18:00
(last entry 17:00)
November to December: 9:00-17:00
(last entry 16:00)
The palace is closed on Tuesdays.

Ticket prices:
Adults (Age 19-64) : 3,000 KRW
(more than 10 people 2,400 KRW
Child (Age 7-18): 1,500 KRW
(more than 10 people 1,200 KRW)
Free: Children under 6, adults over
65, people wearing Hanbok, the last
Wednesday of every month (Culture day)

In 2020, The Tonight Show Starring Jimmy Fallon aired a weeklong special called 'BTS Week.' The special started on September 28th and stretched itself over 5 nights. To kick off the week of performances, BTS performed "Idol" in front of Gyeongbokgung's Geunjeongjeon Hall while wearing traditional Korean clothes (hanbok) on September 29th.

Gyeongbokgung is one of the most popular tourist destinations. Around the palace there are rental shops where you can get a hanbok for the day. Not only is it an opportunity to see the set for BTS's performance, but it also lets you discover Korea's history. One of the main charming points is the palace's location. Surrounded by large, modern business buildings Gyeongbokgung visualizes the harmony of old and new. This also made it the perfect stage for BTS's performance of "Idol," since the song integrates a lot of traditional elements in a modern way. At the time of releasing "Idol," they received criticism saying that they were 'too westernized.' As a response, BTS used traditional sounds in the song, wore traditional clothes and added a lot of Korean cultural references into the music video, while proudly telling the world that "you can't stop me loving myself." This makes this iconic performance all the more meaningful, as they have risen even higher since the release of that song and are ultimately embracing their Korean identity, while sharing their culture with the rest of the world.

On October 2nd, they returned to the palace for a performance of "Mikrokosmos" in front of the Gyeonghoeru Pavilion during 'BTS Week.' Also on October 2nd, BTS released on their Youtube channel a performance of "Dynamite" they did wearing the same hanboks from their "Idol" performance and in the same location. This performance

Gyeongbokgung

Gyeongbokgung

shows the comedic sides of the members as later in the song we see RM and V in the background pretending to attack each other with swords, Jin and Jimin end up doing deep bows in their choreography, and most of the members try hard not to break into laughter at each other's antics. This shows their versatility in being professional, charismatic and down-to-earth while emphasizing how far they, and Korea, have come over the years.

161, Sajik-ro, Jongno-gu
서울 종로구 사직로 161
Gyeongbokgung Station 경복궁역, Exit 5 (line 3)

#Performance

Woonkyung Gotaek 운경고택

Opening hours: Varying opening hours and programs

Entrance fees: Might vary according to programs

Check website in advance for more detailed information
(https://woonkyung.or.kr)

This is the house of Woon Kyung, also known as Lee Jae-hyung, a former chairman of the National Assembly, who lived here in the 1960s until he passed away in 1992. The house is a hanok (traditional Korean house) and operates cultural and artistic programs. The exhibition that RM shared photos of on his official instagram on May 21st, 2022 was an exhibition called, "Woonkyung Gotaek's Spring Spring Spring" created by Choi Jeong-Hwa. The exhibition ran from April 15th to June 17th and uses everyday crafts that harmonize with the preexisting space of the house. It presented a new experience in which modern history and personal history met each other. The place itself is an inconspicuous building up on a slight hill next to Sajik Park. The area makes for a nice little walk and is only a 20 minute walk away from Gyeongbokgung.

7, Inwangsan-ro, Jongno-gu
서울 종로구 인왕산로 7
Gyeongbokgung Station 경복궁역, Exit 1 (line 3)

Yoon Dong-Ju Literary House

Yoon Dong-Ju Literary House

Yoon Dong-Ju Literary House
윤동주문학관

"Until the day I die
I long to have no speck of shame
When I gaze up toward heaven"
- Yoon Dong-Ju, Prologue

Just as England has Shakespeare, Korea has Yoon Dong-Ju. He is one of the most important figures in Korea, someone you should know if you want to understand the nation's collective identity. Koreans have a lot of love and devotion for their country. Yoon Dong-Ju is historically known for his nationalism. His best known works are his resistance poetry, and Yoon is arguably the most important figure when talking about peaceful resistance and love for the motherland since a lot

of Korean identity connects with this poet. He was born in Jiandao, or Kando in Korean, a historical area with Korean settlement ties. Throughout his life, he moved around between China, Korea and Japan. He was later arrested in Japan for allegedly participating in anti-Japanese movements and died in a Japanese prison in 1945 at the age of 27. His poems were critical of Japanese colonialism and often involved a lot of self-reflection. The defining characteristic of his poetry was a sense of bitter longing and love for his homeland. During that time, many educated people went to Japan for their studies because it was the best education available at the time, but even there, they were second-class citizens. His poetry reflects the longing for home and the sense of shame these people felt for being part of the intelligentsia/resistance. His poetry evokes feelings of empathy and compassion. He has become the messenger of resistance and a symbol of courage to overcome one's anxieties. Even in contemporary culture, he continues to inspire younger generations. He has become the hero for the generations who suffer from the injustices of society.

It's no surprise then that the literature loving RM, who loves to share his favorite books with ARMY and often posts self-reflective texts and photos on social media, would share a photo of himself walking up the scenic hill behind the Yoon Dong-Ju Literary House.

The museum is located up a hill, away from the busy part of Jongno. There is

no subway station, so unless you want to climb the hill, you need to take a bus (lines 1020, 7022 and 7212 stop here). Right next to the museum are some of the hiking trails for Bugaksan (북악산), the mountain north of Gyeongbokgung. The Yoon Dong-Ju Literary House is a museum that exhibits some of his original handwritten manuscripts. They also do screenings of a video explaining Yoon Dong-Ju's life and work, but it's entirely in Korean and does not have English subtitles, so that might be less interesting for those unfamiliar with the language. It is a fun stop for anyone that shares RM's passion for literature and poetry. There is also a little outdoor cafe behind the museum, where you can

Daeo Bookstore/Café

have a drink in the shade of the trees and enjoy the quiet atmosphere. The small hill behind the house and its surrounding grounds offers a beautiful view of Seoul by day or night.

119, Changuimun-ro, Jongno-gu
서울 종로구 창의문로 119
no subway
Bus lines 1020, 7022, 7212

#SNS

Daeo Bookstore/Café 대오서점

Jongno is a busy district with a lot of Koreans and tourists always out and about, but this bookstore-café is in a lovely little alley away from the usual hustle of busy Seoul. Located to the west of Gyeongbokgung, there are fewer tourists that stray off into this part of Jongno. The alley is more residential, with a few cafes, smaller local stores and hairdressers decorating the streets. The bookstorecafe's old and run-down storefront is noticeable and inconspicuous at the same time. The main charm of this little old café, which opened in 1951, is exactly this feeling of nostalgia and forgotten times.

There is a certain homey feeling and familiarity, amplified by the narrowness of the rooms. As such, the cafe would not appeal to big groups, but is perfect for small gatherings among close friends. The collection of old books and photographs that decorate the walls hold the history of generations.

It is no wonder then that RM, known for his love for books, is amongst the many guests that have visited this store. The little back courtyard, surrounded with more rooms reminiscent of past times is also the famous location of the photos RM once shared with the world. It is also where you can find his signature along with other celebrities. This place is perfect for people who enjoy coffee booklovers and those who are fascinated in the history of things.

55, Jahamun-ro 7gil, Jongno-gu
서울 종로구 자하문로 7길 55
Gyeongbokgung Station 경복궁역, Exit 2
(line 3)

#SNS

Donuimun Museum Village
돈의문박물관마을

Opening hours: 10:00-19:00
Closed every Monday

Entrance free

Donuimun Museum Village was the setting for Run BTS! episodes 120-121, in which Detective Jin had to deduce which

Donuimun Museum Village

Donuimun Museum Village

one of the 6 villagers was responsible for destroying the precious ARMY stone. The village is a regeneration village located near Seodaemun Gate (서대문). With its longstanding houses and narrow alleys reminiscent of the past before many redevelopments demolished and reconstructed whole areas in Seoul, it stands witness to modern Seoul's development. But it does more than preserve the past. It's an interactive space where younger generations can glimpse what Seoul was like in the 60s, 70s, and 80s. As the museum village has turned into a space reminiscent of the past, it also fits the retro style of BTS Grammy-nominated single "Dynamite."

Among the buildings in the village is RM's movie theater, a reinterpretation of cinemas in the 1960s through 1980s. Here you can enjoy a little movie and look at the old ticket booth, snack bar and walls decorated with movie posters. In SUGA's vintage photo studio, you can have your photo taken as a souvenir, both in color and black and white. There's also Jung Kook's game arcade, where you can play on the retro game machines. On the second floor of that building is a comic library in which the boys looked for clues and where you can have a look at some vintage comics. Other areas, such as j-hope's hair salon and the doctor's house,

are also accessible and offer insight into what life was like back in the 60s to 80s. As this village is more like an interactive museum, it is suitable for all ages and perfectly combines playfulness with BTS and Korean history.

14-3, Songwol-gil, Jongno-gu
서울 종로구 송월길 14-3
Seodaemun Station 서대문역, Exit 4 (line 5)

#RunBTS

Line Friends (BT21)

49, Insadonggil, Jongno-gu
서울 종로구 인사동길 49
Anguk Station 안국역, Exit 6 (line 3)

#Shopping

Line Friends (BT21)

Mapo-gu

Neighborhoods

Mapo-gu

—

World Cup Bridge

Haneul (Sky) Park

Nanji Hangang Park

Yeonnam Mill Cafe

Rolling Hall

Yeouido Hangang Park

Seokjin Forest

Osseu Seiromushi Yeouido Branch

Abandoned Swimming Pool SNU

Gocheok Skydome

Korea University Hwajeong Gymnasium

Birthday Events

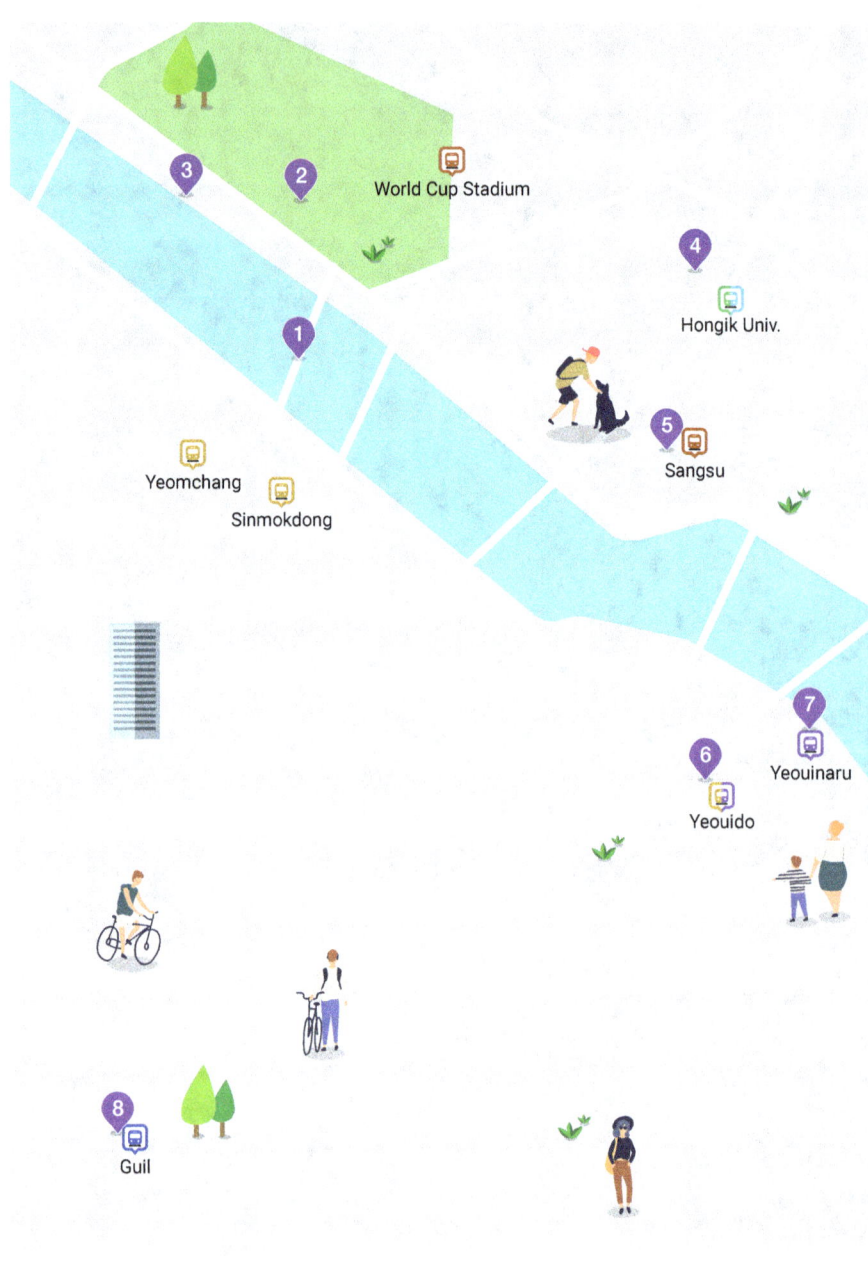

World Cup Stadium

Hongik Univ.

Yeomchang

Sinmokdong

Sangsu

Yeouinaru

Yeouido

Guil

1 World Cup Bridge
2 Haneul (Sky) Park
3 Nanji Hangang Park
4 Yeonnam Mill Cafe

5 Rolling Hall
6 Yeouido
7 Seokjin Forest
8 Gocheok Skydome

Mapo-gu
마포구

Mapo-gu is in the west of Seoul, north of the river. It is one of the hippest areas in Seoul, thanks to the student areas of Sinchon and Hongdae. Even if this is your first time in Korea, you may have heard of Hongdae before because it's one of the most popular areas among younger people. There's plenty of bargain shopping, restaurants and cafes and a busy nightlife around here.

World Cup Bridge 월드컵대교

This bridge stretches over the Han River, connecting Mapo-gu, Yeongdeungpo-gu and Yangcheon-gu. The bridge is a real eye-catcher with its asymmetric cable construction onto which colorful lights shine. On July 15th, 2021, it became a stage for BTS to perform. As a part of a two-night musical special on The Tonight Show starring Jimmy Fallon, where they also made the U.S. television debut of "Permission to Dance," BTS delivered a unique performance of "Butter" on this bridge. The construction of this bridge started in 2010, but it was delayed because of issues with the budget. It opened on September 1st, 2021, so the

World Cup Bridge

Hongdae culture & special tourist zone

bridge had not officially been completed yet at the time of their performance.

Haneul (Sky) Park 하늘공원

On one of his days off in nature, RM went for a walk here in Haneul Park, one of the most popular parks in Seoul. The name 'Haneul' translates to 'sky', which is fitting for this park that is slightly elevated and gives you a beautiful view of Seoul and the Han River. It is especially pretty in October when the silver grass is in full bloom. It is a very popular spot to take photos in front of the pink grass.

The park is located in the World Cup Park which commemorates the 17th FIFA World Cup. The park used to be a beautiful island popular amongst couples to go on dates but in 1978 was then turned into a landfill up until the mid-90s. This had a negative effect on nature and the people living around the place, so the Seoul Metropolitan government decided to turn it back into an ecological park. Today it is one of the most popular recreational spaces.

Getting up to the park is a bit of a workout though, there are 291 steps that you need to climb. Especially on a warm summer day, you will need some good sunscreen and a bottle of water.

95, Haneulgongwon-ro, Mapo-gu
서울 마포구 하늘공원로 95
World Cup Stadium Station
월드컵경기장역, Exit 1 (line 6)

#SNS

Nanji Hangang Park 난지한강공원

Unveiled in April 2023 is the BTS Forest in the Nanji Han River Park on the western side of Seoul. Melon, a mainstream music streaming service in Korea, were the ones to establish the bench using money donated by their subscribers as part of their project's initiative. BTS are the first artists, both domestic and international, to have enough money donated through Melon to warrant a forest. The BTS Forest is not far from Haneul Park (하늘공원) and consists of a bench, three fringe trees and 400 sacred bamboo trees. You can search 'Bangtan Sonyeondan Sup' (방탄소년단숲) in your navigation app or walk from Haneul Park by heading towards the river.

162, Hangangnanji-ro, Mapo-gu
서울 마포구 한강난지로 162
no subway
Bus lines 401, 402, 9711

Yeonnam Mill Cafe

Yeonnam Mill Cafe 연남방앗간

In the area of Yeonnam there is an oasis of unique cafés, vintage stores and older architecture buildings. One café that is a hidden treasure is Yeonnam Mill that overlooks the Gyeongui Line Forest Park (경의선숲길공원), a beautiful feature that runs through a large part of Hongdae. Walking into this curated space you will be in awe over the classy vibe of the place. The walls, floor and even ceiling consist of dark, rich wood and a majestic chandelier hangs in the center. There is a grand staircase and wall made of shelves that are especially worth noting as they featured in a BTS photoshoot.

In 2020 BTS were the cover stars for WSJ Magazine's Innovator issue as the company's music innovator of the year. For their individual photos they dressed in dark suits and positioned themselves around the main room of the cafe. In their group shots they remove their jackets and pose in front of the wall bookcase. If you go today the layout of the furniture is different, but these elements from the photos are almost identical. The lighting in this cafe is very soft and feels special, making it an understandable pick for an elegant photoshoot.

The café's menu is fairly limited, but the coffee is excellent quality. This café also specializes in sesame flavor: it has a sesame latte that is their signature and sells sesame oil in bottles.

34, Donggyo-ro 29gil, Yeonnam-dong, Mapo-gu 서울 마포구 동교로 29길 34

Hongik Univ. Station 홍대입구역, Exit 3
(line 2, Airport line)

Rolling Hall 롤링홀

Rolling Hall is a famous performance venue in Hongdae founded in 1995 and has legendary status. Hundreds of renowned artists, both Korean and international, have performed here. The concert hall is small with only a capacity for 400 people, which makes the events held here more intimate in feel. On December 5th, three days after releasing his debut solo album Indigo, RM hosted a private concert with 200 raffle-winning ARMYs. Recorded live, "RM Live in Seoul @ Rolling Hall" was later shared on the BangtanTV Youtube channel for everyone to enjoy. The concert saw RM perform with many of the featured artists on Indigo, such as Paul Blanco, Colde, Kim Sawol and youjeen from Cherry Filter. Many of the performances from this night are now considered iconic and shared often online.

To see inside the venue you will need a ticket to a concert, but the venue is often hosting various artists. You can visit their website (http://www.rollinghall.co.kr/default) to see which artists are having concerts and find out for yourself why RM describes Rolling Hall as "my dream concert hall."

35, Eoulmadang-ro, Mapo-gu
서울 마포구 어울마당로 35
Sangsu Station 상수역, Exit 1 (line 6)

Rolling Hall

Yeouido 여의도

Yeouido is an island located on the edge of the Han River to the south-west of Seoul. It is in between Noryangjin and Yeongdeungpo, and is across the river from Mapo-gu. This area is the business and banking center of Seoul, so if you visit, expect to see many people dressed in business attire and running to and from meetings. Yeouido is most popular with tourists for the Yeouido Hangang Park that hosts the Seoul Fireworks festival at the end of summer every year, the ELand River Cruise and the main Hyundai Seoul mall, the largest shopping mall in Seoul equivalent in size to 13 football fields. It is a popular destination in the summer evenings and weekends for picnics, busking and exercising.

Yeouido Hangang Park 한강공원

This park is one of the most popular along the Han River and is easy to access thanks to the Yeouinaru Station (여의나루역) there. It offers scenic views of Seoul including the golden Seoul 63 building, surrounding Mapo Bridge (마포대교) and Wonhyo Bridge (원효대교), as well as N Seoul Tower in the distance. The park offers shade and shallow wading pools in summer, cherry blossoms in spring, sparkling Christmas lights in winter and bright yellow ginkgo trees in the fall. It is very easy to spend an afternoon or evening picnicking here as there are various market food stalls, picnic mat and seat rentals and a convenience store.

On June 17th, 2023 Yeouido Hangang Park became the center of the BTS 10 year anniversary Festa as it hosted a one day event. The park overflowed with purple decorations, booths, displays and activities related to BTS for ARMY to enjoy. There were photo galleries for each year of Festa, a wall showcasing various trophies BTS have won and the

outfits BTS performed "Run BTS" for the first time live at the 'Yet To Come' concert in Busan the year before. Many ARMYs converged around the outdoor cinema screens set up to show music videos and performances throughout the day. This is also where people could watch the special event held by RM that day in the park if they did not win the raffle. For those lucky enough to win the raffle, there was a special 'ARMY Lounge' that held 3,000 seats for RM's one and a half hour show, 'It's 5pm and This is Kim Namjun.'

During this show RM performed two songs, "Intro: Persona" and "Wildflower," and read out stories sent in by ARMY in funny voices. He also took a quiz with ARMY and received two special phone calls from fellow members Jung Kook and V. The festival concluded officially with a fireworks display that night which matched explosions with a medley of BTS songs. It was so impressive that people could see and hear it all over Seoul. Unofficially, the festival finished hours later after ARMY held a dance party in the park with all their lightsticks. In total, 400,000 people showed up to Yeouido Hangang Park for the festival that day. And in typical fashion, ARMY received praise from RM and local media for leaving the park spotless when they left. Once again reminding the world what a great - and well-respected fandom we are.

Jin Forest

Seokjin Forest 석진숲

Inside Yeouido Hangang Park is Jin forest. In December 2022, as a birthday project, 500 ARMY gathered with the Seoul Environmental Federation to create the first Jin Forest in Seoul. Next to four dedicated benches are 10 horse chestnut trees with signs naming them after Jin's solo songs and attached with QR codes that directly link to the songs to make listening to them easy.

To get to Jin forest you can search 'Seokjin Forest' or '석진숲' in your navigation app. Or you can go to Yeouinaru station (여의나루역) and use exit 2. This will lead you to the central plaza of Yeouido Park. You will need to go down the steps towards the river. Before you go down the

second set of stairs near the boardwalk you will find a path to your right. You should see a black, rounded building with yellow edging. Head in this direction and along the way you will find Jin's forest on your right, with great views of the Han River to your left.

85-6, Yeouido-dong, Yeongdeungpo-gu
서울 영등포구 여의도동 85-6
Yeouinaru Station 여의나루역, Exit 3 (line 5)

Osseu Seiromushi Yeouido Branch 오쓰 세이로무시 여의도

After the success of his Songpa restaurant, Jin's brother opened a second branch of the restaurant located in Yeouido. This restaurant has a slightly altered menu,

Osseu Seiromushi Yeouido Branch

though it does still specialize in Japanese style steam cooking for meat, seafood and vegetables. This establishment has a sophisticated gallery vibe to it. There is art displayed in the restaurant and no windows to look inside making it a private place to enjoy a meeting or meal. The restaurant is also located in the basement of the building. From the front, you will see a set of staircases that lead down. Upon entering through the glass doors, you will encounter the dark marble entrance of Osseu Seiromushi.

On the day of Jin's enlistment, j-hope posted to his Instagram stories photos of him and Jin together, including a meal shared at this restaurant. The table is predictably full of delicious food, including the restaurant's signature bamboo tray menu items.

Bookings are recommended to eat at this restaurant and easy to do online or through the Naver app.

B1, 36, Gukjegeumyung-ro 2gil, Yeongdeungpo-gu 서울 영등포구 국제금융로 2길 36
B1 Yeouido Station 여의도역, Exit 3 (line 5, 9)

Other Locations in Seoul

Abandoned Swimming Pool SNU

For many years, the abandoned swimming pool at Seoul National University was one of the most popular places for ARMY to visit on their trips to Korea. It was the set for the majority of the '화양연화 on stage: prologue' video released in October 2015, five months after the release of "I NEED U." In 2020, SNU officially decided to demolish the pool stating management and safety reasons. At the time, some financial issues put the demolition on hold, but in 2021 removal of the abandoned pool eventually went ahead. However, part of one wall remains preserved and possible to visit. While not the full experience of the music video, or what was available years ago, the recognition of the pool's significance and its maintenance for ARMY is wonderful.

Abandoned Swimming Pool SNU

The pool is meaningful for a couple of reasons. It already existed at Gwanak Mountain before Seoul University moved its campus to Gwanak Campus in 1975 and continued to operate after the university settled. The university used the pool until the 1980s, despite its secluded location and cold water temperatures. In the 1980s, after the May 18 Gwangju Democratic Uprising started, the student movements spread nationwide. At that time, students in Seoul used to hide around this pool to avoid the police. Gwangju is j-hope's hometown and he references this event in the lyrics to "Ma City," when he says, "Everyone press 062-518." The 062 here stands for the regional telephone code for Gwangju, and 518 (오일팔) is how Koreans refer to this event.

In the early 1990s, it ultimately closed but soon drew attention from other people and transformed into a cultural space. Before its demolition, this old pool complex became popular with BTS fans, graffiti artists, fashion photographers, and movie makers. Its eerie vibe and the luscious greenery made it the perfect set for all kinds of visual art projects. Besides the pool, there was an old bathhouse/sauna that BTS also used as a filming set.

The prologue begins with V whose character in the parallel universe (strong emphasis here! This is a fictional character in a fictional setting and by no means refers to the real V himself) kills his father and calls his friends. They are then seen hanging out by the abandoned pool together, goofing around and enjoying their time while the instrumentals for "Butterfly (Prologue Mix)" plays in the background. Through this 12-minute video, BTS perfectly captured what it feels like as a young adult plagued with anxieties and uncertainties but who finds comfort through their friends. They couldn't have found a better location to film this video, since the abandoned pool helped add to the intense visual effect that the video has on the viewer.

Most ARMYs have been dismayed by the decision to demolish so much of this location, as it held many dear memories for ARMY, who found comfort and peace in that particularly profound era of BTS. There's a certain irony in this, however. The pool itself has now become a memory that gives you the same bittersweet feeling of pain and happiness that The Most Beautiful Moment In Life era gave us.

This remaining piece of the pool is small, but for many will still be worth visiting. It is a longer traveling distance than the Seoul items listed so far, but still manageable by an hour ride on public transport. You can search 'Seoul National University Gwanak Campus Swimming Pool' (서울대학교 관악캠퍼스 수영장) on your navigation app of choice. You will need to pass through a parking lot and climb a wooded series of stone steps to reach the area. Though the climb is short and the steps well

maintained, they will be difficult if you have mobility issues, so please be careful. The area is a charming dedication to what used to be the swimming pool, with now only one wall preserved and a paved area with benches. As it's higher up, it has a nice breeze and mountain views around. It's an ideal place for a picnic, to read a book, or to sit and listen to some music.

1, Gwanak-ro, Gwanak-gu
서울 관악구 관악로 1
Gwanaksan Station 관악산역, Exit 1
(Sinlim line 신림선)

Gocheok Skydome 고척스카이돔

BTS's group name literally translates to 'Bulletproof Boy Scouts' and with the fandom name being ARMY (short for 'Adorable Representative MC for Youth'), it is only logical that they would use a matching term to refer to their fan meetings. In this case, they went for 'Muster', which means a formal gathering of troops. This venue is where they held two of those fan meetings. The Skydome has a capacity of around 25,000 people for concerts. This venue is quite special because it's the birthplace of BTS and ARMY's most meaningful slogan.

The first time they ever performed in this venue was for the 3rd Muster 'ARMY.ZIP+' in November 2016. On the first day of

Gocheok Skydome

this fan meeting, V opened up about his grandmother passing away. ARMY was moved not only because of the personal story he shared, but also because he showed how much trust he has in the fans. In a way, it was yet another example of the strong bond between BTS and ARMY. On the second day, V created the phrase ' 보라해' (borahae/ I purple you). During their performance of "2!3!" ARMY surprised them by covering their lightsticks (called ARMYbomb) with something purple. At the time, they didn't have the function to change colors yet, so the members were really taken by surprise. Jung Kook even joked saying he thought something was wrong with his eyes and j-hope compared it to blooming flowers. V asked the crowd if they knew what the color purple means,

explaining that it is the last color of the rainbow and it means, "I will trust and love you for a very long time," admitting that he just made that up on the spot. Everyone loved the phrase so much that it has since become like an official slogan for BTS and ARMY. It also goes beyond the group and the fandom now. In 2018, UNICEF released a clip in celebration of reaching over 1 million dollars for the 'Love Myself' campaign that they launched in 2017 together with BTS. They used the hashtag 'IPurpleYou' and UNICEF executive director Henrietta H. Fore ended the video with the words, "We here at UNICEF purple you!" In 2021, BTS collaborated with McDonald's for the 'BTS Meal' who used the phrase 'borahae' to decorate the purple chicken McNugget packaging and cups.

They later came back to Gocheok Skydome for their 4th Muster, 'Happy Ever After,' in January 2018. In between, they returned here for their 'BTS Live Trilogy Episode III The Wings Tour' in February 2017 and for the final of the same tour in December 2017. At the end of the final 'Wings' show, they were flying around the venue in rainbow-colored hot-air balloons, taking their time to look at every single ARMY. Jimin has mentioned on numerous occasions how much he loves making eye contact with the fans, and in recent interviews, the members often said that looking at the people in the audience is what they miss the most. It is also a cute idea to have the members fly around the venue while singing "Outro: Wings" as they leave.

430, Gyeongin-ro, Guro-gu
서울 구로구 경인로 430
Guil Station 구일역, Exit 2 (line 1)

Korea University Hwajeong Gymnasium 고려대학교 화정체육관

Their second anniversary fan meeting Muster was originally scheduled for June 2015 under the title ZIP CODE 17520. They had to cancel the event four days before, on June 9th, because of the MERS outbreak. It was later held in January 2016 under the title ZIP CODE 22920.

48, Gaeunsa 2gil, Seongbuk-gu
서울 성북구 개운사 2길 48
A nam Station 안암역, Exit 1(line 6)

Birthday Events

For a detailed explanation on what birthday events are, please refer to the definition in the 'Things to Know' section (see page 170).

It can be overwhelming and impossible to catch up with every single event. They are not only limited to Seoul but also held in other cities. Since ARMY loves to express their love for every member, there are generally hundreds of different events, advertisements, and installations in Seoul alone. The best way to discover events near you is to check social media platforms such as Twitter or Instagram beforehand. Type in the member's name, the event you are looking for (advertisement, installation, cup holder event, etc) and your location. There are also websites that you can keep an eye on to help you keep track, for example: https://www.armymap.net (available in Korean, English and Japanese). By clicking on the different locations, you will get basic information of the event period and sometimes even what special birthday set they are selling.

Outside Seoul

Outside Seoul

Il-Yeong Station 일영역 (폐역)

Located about an hour outside of Seoul, this iconic abandoned train station was the setting for the opening of the "Spring Day" music video. Released on February 13h, 2017, "Spring Day" was the title track for their repackaging of the Wings (2106) album, You Never Walk Alone (2017). The song and video for "Spring Day" were often linked to the Sewol Ferry disaster in 2014. In an interview with KBS in November 2020, they revealed that the song is based on personal stories from RM and SUGA. SUGA suggested that everyone would have experienced similar emotions before. RM then explained that he wrote the song while sitting in the park at Han River, followed by a little anecdote about how the demo version he recorded was off-key, prompting laughter from his members. In the same interview, V revealed that he had also submitted a version for this song, but they ended up going with RM's instead. V's demo of "Spring Day" is now available to listen to on CD3 of their physical album Proof (2022). In an interview with Esquire in November 2020, the group was asked

Il-Yeong Station

Dae Jang Geum Park

if the song was about a specific sad incident, to which Jin answered: "It is about a sad event, as you said, but it is also about longing."

The song has been steadily receiving love and kept its spot in the charts over the years. It is commonly known amongst ARMY as 'Queen Spring Day' because the song has never been dethroned from the charts. It has also become a popular joke whenever BTS has a new comeback to pit the two latest releases against each other for their spot on the charts, with a relaxed "Spring Day" chilling in the background stil ranked.

This location itself is in Yangju-si, a little outside of Seoul in a rather quiet area.

If you enter 'Iryeong Station Temporary Station' or '일영역' into your navigation app (especially Naver) you will receive directions on how to get there. Depending where you are coming from within Seoul, the journey will take a minimum of one hour to get there by subway and bus. There are signs on the main road indicating the way to the station. There is not a lot to see in this area though, except for a café near the bus stop that you will be arriving/leaving at.

327, Samsang-ri, Jangheung-myeon, Yangju-si, Gyeonggi-do
경기 양주시 장흥면 삼상리 327

#MusicVideo

Dae Jang Geum Park

Dae Jang Geum Park
용인대장금테마파크

Established in 2005, Dae Jang Geum Park has become the biggest filming site in Korea for historical dramas. In May 2020, it became the set for the "Daechwita" music video by Agust D (SUGA). The song was the title track of his second mixtape D-2 (2020), released four years after his first mixtape Agust D. In the video, the old Agust D has become a mad king and is now facing a new Agust D, both played by SUGA himself. The music video also features guest appearances of fellow members Jin and Jung Kook, who fight in the background as SUGA continues to stroll down the old traditional market. j-hope also visited the set and even sent him a coffee truck to celebrate the occasion.

In an interview, SUGA revealed that he was actively involved in creating the music video. He said that when he met the director in the planning stages, they initially planned for a minimal music video, but he insisted that he wanted to film it at a historical drama set. The reason behind that was he thought it would fit the song and he also liked historical dramas himself. He added that since he often used traditional elements in his songs, he thought he should cut back on that now and wrap it up. For the video, he

also learned a sword dance, for which he had a hwando (a traditional sword from the Joseon era) made by a real sword craftsman. (The dance feature was short in the music video, but a dance practice was later released on YouTube). For the release, he thought it would be fun to surprise fans and drop the mixtape on the D-2 day of the countdown, to match its name and catch fans who are counting down the days off guard.

At Dae Jang Geum Park, visitors can walk the streets of the traditional marketplace, look inside the palace and peruse around the central prison. This is a fun place for anyone who likes "Daechwita," but also fans of historical K-Dramas, or generally people who admire the old Korean aesthetic and its architecture.

The park also sells the gold key with the green accessory SUGA briefly held in the music video. Called Norigae (노리개), which refers to a traditional Korean ornament worn typically by women on the waist as part of their hanbok skirts. They sell it in the store at the entrance and in the café Mia up by Muryangsujeon Hall/Anyagru Pavilion. They cost around 29,900 KRW and are cute little souvenirs or gifts for your friends and family back home or as a keepsake for yourself.

The park is a bit further away from Seoul but is possible as a day trip. To get there, you have to take the bus at Seoul Nambu Bus Terminal (서울남부버스터미널) in Seocho (서초구) to Baekam (백암).

You get off at Baekam Bus Terminal (백암 버스터미널) and either take bus #105 or continue by taxi. The schedule for bus #105 is a bit tricky and does not come in regular intervals, so if you plan on taking the bus all the way, make sure to check the time schedule beforehand. Bus #105 is a shuttle bus between Jirunggol and Yongin Dae Jang Geum Park (sometimes referred to as MBC Set Bus Stop). The following times provided are the departure times at Jirunggol, and it takes the bus about 5 minutes to arrive at Baekam Bus Terminal. It is best to be at Baekam around the time it leaves Jirunggol, just to be safe:

08:25 10:00 13:00 14:55 16:30

Upon your arrival at the park, make sure you check the time schedule for the returning buses back to Baekam, too!

Opening hours:
Summer Season (March - October: 09:00 - 18:00)
Winter Season (November - February 09:00 - 17:00)
The park is open throughout the whole year and you can enter up until one hour before the closing time.

Admission fees:
Adults (age over 19): 9,500 KRW
Middle & High School Students (age 13-18): 8,000 KRW
Children (age 4-12): 7,000 KRW
Preschooler (under 4): Free
Tour car: 3,000 KRW (15 minutes)

25, Yongcheon dramagil, Baegam-myeon, Cheoin-gu, Yongin-si, Gyeonggi-do
경기 용인시 처인구 백암면 용천드라마길 25

#MusicVideo

Everland Amusement Park 에버랜드

Opening hours might vary so please check out their website before your trip.

On September 17th, 2020, BTS performed "Dynamite" on America's Got Talent. They filmed the performance at the American-themed area of Everland Amusement Park. This area of the theme park perfectly fits the feeling and aesthetic they were going for with "Dynamite."

Previously, it was the set for Run BTS! episode 24, in which the boys naively believed they were going on a night safari but instead ended up surprised by zombies. In this episode, full of screaming and scared members, all three teams failed to accomplish the mission, with Jin and SUGA spending most of their time dressing up as zombies to blend in. They only managed to get some free tickets for ARMY through a game of freeze tag with the zombies at the end of the episode.

Everland is the largest theme park in South Korea and includes a little zoo. It is the perfect place for people of all ages to take a day off and enjoy themselves. From Gangnam, it takes approximately an hour by bus from Seoul to get there. If you are traveling from areas such as Hongdae, Myeongdong or Seoul Station, then paying for the shuttle bus is the more convenient option. A shuttle bus round trip ticket can be purchased from sites like Klook or Trazy. You can also purchase packages on these websites that bundle your Everland admission ticket with transfer there and back that are reasonably priced.

Everland is a great place to travel as a day trip, especially with a group. If you travel with fellow ARMY, or make ARMY friends while on your trip, it is worth making the journey here.

199, Everland-ro, Pogok-eup, Cheoin-gu, Yongin-si, Gyeonggi-do
경기도 용인시 처인구 포곡읍 에버랜드로 199

#Performance, #RunBTS

Lee Jaehyo Gallery 이재효 갤러리

Both Lee Jaehyo Gallery and the Museum San are not really accessible by public transport, but if you plan on renting a car, you should absolutely plan some time to visit these places. On January 20th, 2022, RM posted photos of himself at the Lee Jaehyo Gallery to his personal Instagram. The gallery stretches itself over five different exhibition halls, featuring sculptures, paintings, and furniture. There is also a café with a beautiful view of the scenery surrounding the gallery, which is in a rather remote area. You can buy an entrance ticket that includes a drink, so once you're done admiring the art, you can recharge while admiring nature.

The gallery is open year-round between 10AM and 6PM (last entry is at 5PM). Be sure to make a reservation before journeying to the gallery.

83-22, Chocheongil, Jipyeong-myeon, Yangpyeong-gun, Gyeonggi-do
경기도 양평군 지평면 초천길 83-22

#SNS

Museum San 뮤지엄 산

Similar to the Lee Jaehyo Gallery, this museum is hard to reach using public transport, but a total must-see if you can rent a car and drive around the country. In August 2019, RM shared photos of himself at this museum to the group's official Twitter account, captioned with a mountain emoji (the Korean word for mountain is san 산, just like the name of the museum, which is located on a mountain). The museum features multiple indoor exhibition halls, a meditation hall, a beautiful café terrace, and a print studio that offers hands-on programs. Besides the exhibitions, the museum's architecture and scenic location make it feel like a real getaway experience in nature.

The museum is open all-year round from 10AM to 6PM, and there are various types of tickets, packages and tours so it is best to check the website before planning your visit.

Museum San website:

http://www.museumsan.org/eng/

260, Oak valley 2gil, Jijeong-myeon, Wonju-si, Gangwon-do
강원도 원주시 지정면 오크밸리 2길 260

#SNS

Lake 192 레이크192

Most ARMYs will know the show BTS In The Soop with its catchy yet serene theme song. The members filmed two seasons over the course of the pandemic when international travel was not possible. The concept of the show is to film the members on a 'staycation,' doing activities they normally never indulge in while relaxing and bonding with each other. They filmed the first season at this Lake house in Chuncheon, where the members stayed for a week. What is amazing is that this place is available for you to stay on AirBnB.

Nestled between mountains and Bukhan River (북한강), is Lake 192, where the first season is set. The property contains the 'Main House': the two storey, two bedroom property that is modern in design. This includes the master bedroom RM stayed in which hosts a stunning bathroom with floor to ceiling window in the shower and a great view of the yard and surrounding mountains. There is also the 'Upper House' which is a one-storey, two bedroom accommodation that the BigHit Producers modified to be the gaming hub. This is also where Jimin slept and the location of the rustic style kitchen. Finally, there is the 'Floating House,' a two bedroom guest house that floats on the river and connects to land by a wooden walkway. This is where Jung Kook slept and where Jin, SUGA and Jung Kook all went fishing more than once throughout the show. The campervan that SUGA stays in, and writes music for his D2 and D-Day albums as shown in his Disney+ documentary SUGA: Road to D-Day, is also on the property but is not available to stay in.

Lake 192

While the producers of the show modified the accommodation to suit both the members and filming needs, much of the location is easily recognizable. Not just that, the property's design emphasizes relaxing and enjoying the surrounding nature. In fact, the house won a 'Korea Architecture Prize' and appears in other shows and commercials. It is also a popular destination for workshops, retreats and small weddings. It is then not a surprise that it can be difficult to book a stay here, nor is it cheap.

If you stay for one night at Lake 192 you can expect to check in around 3pm and stay until 11am the next day. The 'Main House' and 'Floating House' are the main sleeping quarters, though the bedrooms and outdoor space of the 'Upper House' are usually available to you as well. If you can find the availability, then longer stays are also an option here. Since the price tag is hefty, many ARMYs prefer to organize group stays. There is a boat and a karaoke machine that you can use, plus art supplies and campfire equipment too. For an additional cost, you can also hire kayaks. The host is a very friendly, gracious woman who speaks decent English and knows how to take good photos for you and your companions.

To get to Lake 192 is also not a straight-forward process. The easiest method is to hire a car and drive yourself. From Seoul this is a 2.5 - 3 hour drive through beautiful mountainous countryside. Another option is to take the KTX to Namchuncheon Station and then catch a 40 minute taxi ride. Though it is not convenient, it does make the remoteness of Lake 192 all the more special to visitors.

192-3, Gail-ri Sabuk-myeon, Chuncheon-si, Gangwon-do
강원도 춘천시 사북면 가일리 192-3

In The Soop 2

The setting for Season 2 of In The Soop is in Pyeongchang, in the same Gangwon province as the first season house, but is much more private. Rather than rent another space, HYBE purchased the land and had it landscaped and the properties remodeled. Now this location has 3 two-storey villas (referred to in the show as 'House A', 'House B' and 'House C'), a swimming pool, a basketball court, a tennis court and a camping zone.

Beyond being the set for BTS In The Soop season 2, this location appears once again in SUGA's Disney+ documentary SUGA: Road to D-Day. In the documentary, while struggling with creating his D-Day album SUGA goes back to the Pyeongchang Soop house with various musicians and producers to do a music camp and work through his creative block. He seems to relax, get pensive, and have fun there, and

it must have helped as he released his D-Day album in April 2023 and broke some of the biggest records for a rap artist ever.

The property remained elusive until late July 2022, when a listing for the In The Soop Season 2 house appeared on AirBnB. A special day was being marketed for two guests to stay overnight for $7. This, understandably, increased interest in the location and how one could see it for themselves. Now 1.5 hour tours are available of the house where you can freely roam around, see some of the decorations from the show (SUGA's guitar, Bam's dog mat and j-hope's paper plane are all on display), take pictures in the special photobooth and get exclusive merch at its store.

There are multiple tour packages offered online to tour the In The Soop season 2 house, and some add other BTS locations in the area. These tours include the transport to and from Pyeongchang which is useful as it is still a difficult area to get to with public transport. Another option is to stay at the nearby Phoenix Hotel Pyeongchang, which offers as a package the 1.5 hour tour of the In the Soop house.

Pyeongchang-gun, Gangwon Province
강원도 평창군

Day Trip

Ilsan

—

Goyang Tourist Center

La Festa and Western Dome

Lake Park

One Mount

Hugok Academy Village

Sinil Middle School

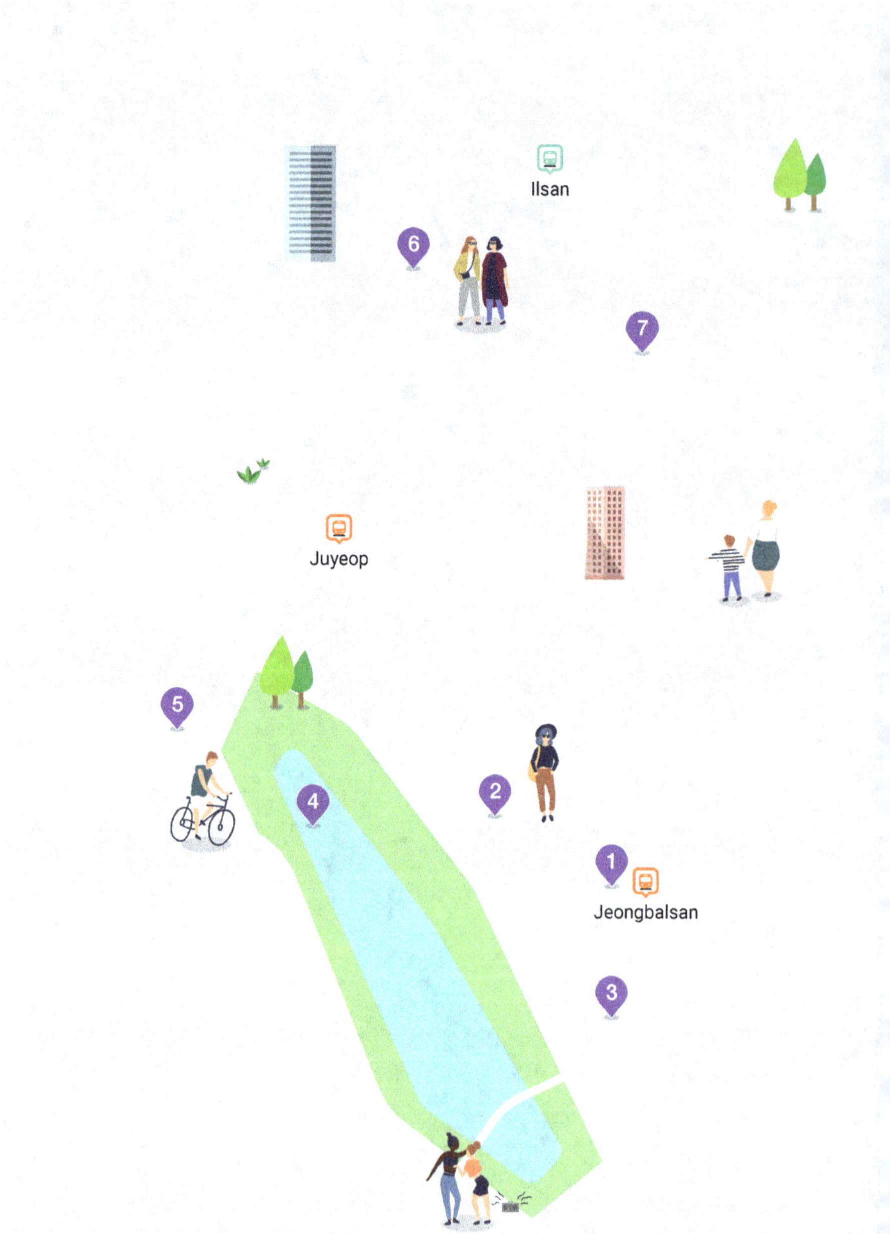

Ilsan

Juyeop

Jeongbalsan

1 Goyang Tourist Center

2 La Festa

3 Western Dome

4 Lake Park

5 One Mount

6 Hugok Academy Village

7 Sinil Middle School

Ilsan
일산

"Ilsan - the place where I want to be buried even after I die, it's the city of the flower, city of Mon" - Ma City, The Most Beautiful Moment In Life: Young Forever

An hour north-west of Seoul is the town of Ilsan inside the Goyang province. Ilsan is a satellite city, or an area man-made to alleviate housing shortages in Seoul. Ilsan has developed into a bustling but peaceful town full of greenery and unique architecture. It is now also known for being the hometown of BTS leader, RM. As it is very easy and affordable to get to, Ilsan is a great place to visit as a day trip.

How to get there

Ilsan is less than an hour away by subway for most locations in Seoul. You can take line 3 to Jeongbalsan Station (정발산역). Or take the Gyeongui-Jungang Line(경의 중앙) and get off at Pungsan (풍산) Station.

Goyang Tourist Center
고양관광정보센터

If you take exit 1 from Jeongbalsan Station you will be within a minute's walk of the Goyang Tourist Center. This is perfect because this is the location of the stunning RM mural created for his 28th birthday, unveiled in September 2021. The mural has RM clutching his blue microphone with flowers and a cat

Goyang Tourist Center

Goyang Tourist Center

around him, both to represent Goyang (goyangi is the Korean word for cat). RM has expressed his love for Ilsan countless times, from his lyrics in "Ma City," to his powerful 2018 UN speech, and so the city wanted to celebrate him by teaming up with an online fangroup to fund this art-piece as a tourist attraction, hence its location at the tourist center.

The city is so proud of RM that in November 2019 the Goyang City Youtube channel uploaded a BTS dance medley highlighting all the spots in Ilsan that connect to RM, including the places mentioned in his "Ma City" lyrics, such as Western Dome, the Hugok Academy Village, and his middle school, to name

just a few. As most of these locations are all close in distance to each other, you can see them all in your day trip too.

At the mural there are also benches signed by fellow ARMYs who have come to visit the mural. While looking at the mural face-on, do not miss the second mural behind you under the staircase. Here RM's verse from "Ma City" glimmers on the ceiling with a background of a galaxy. The scale alone of these murals is truly impressive.

845, Janghang-dong, Ilsandong-gu, Goyang-si, Gyeonggi-do
경기 고양시 일산동구 장항동 845

La Festa 라페스타 and Western Dome 웨스턴돔

"Lafesta and Western Dome that felt like home" - Ma City

La Festa and Western Dome are essentially the same things and are next to each other. This is why we are combining them in this guide as if you follow the street you will walk through both of them, with the Tourist Information Center located in the middle of them. La Festa and Western Dome are socializing hubs for the youth of Ilsan, especially the students. They are essentially open malls, with streets full of cafes, restaurants, fashion outlets, arcades, bars and other activities to do. You can think of them as a more laid-back and younger version of Hongdae in Seoul. La Festa is more for middle and highschoolers, whereas Western Dome seems to cater more to university age students. It's not hard to imagine a young middle-schooler RM walking down these streets with his friends years ago. The neighborhood clearly meant something special to him to be included in his lyrics about his hometown.

La Festa

1305-56, Jungang-ro, Ilsandong-gu, Goyang-si, Gyeonggi-do
경기도 고양시 일산동구 중앙로 1305-56

Western Dome

24, Jeongbalsan-ro 42beongil, Ilsandong-gu, Goyang-si, Gyeonggi-do
경기도 고양시 일산동구 정발산로 42번길 24

Lake Park 호수공원

Less than ten minutes walk from La Festa and Western Dome is the Ilsan Lake Park. Most famous for the annual Goyang International Flower Festival, Ilsan has gained nationwide attention for its beautiful flower displays. The Lake Park is one of the largest man-made parks in Asia as it stretches over 900,000 square meters, or 73 acres. The park is excellent to walk around as there are fields, fountains, pavilions and gardens

Lake Park

2023
고양국제꽃박람회
International Horticulture Goyang Korea
일산호수공원
Ilsan Lake Park
2023.4.27–5.8

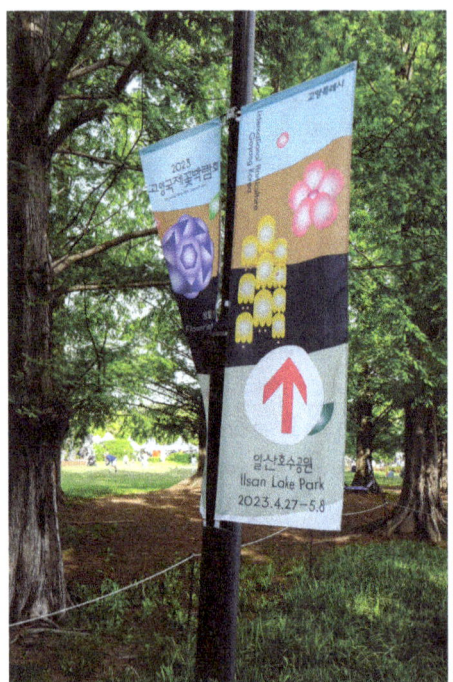

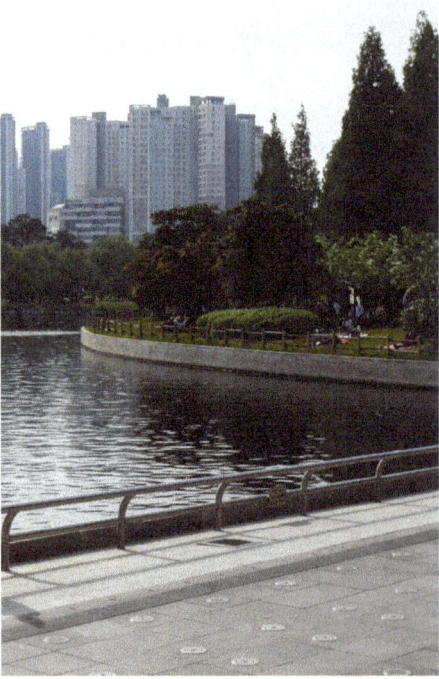

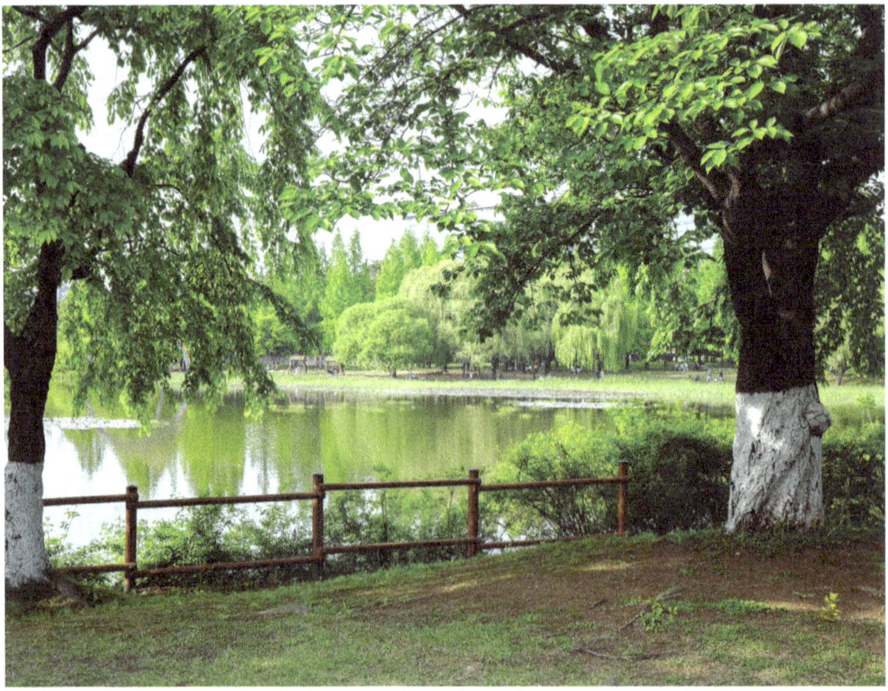

Lake Park

to explore. Alternatively, you can lay out a blanket and enjoy a lazy picnic or nap while looking out across the glass-like lake surface. At night the lake reflects the lights from Ilsan's skyline serenely, making this park a perfect place to be any time of day.

RM has posted countless photos here over the years, including a video of him with a tiny green frog in his hand. In his lyrics describing Ilsan he said, "I like Lake Park more than Han River." The Ilsan Lake Park is a must-see if you come to Ilsan, so prepare to spend a few hours here.

731, Hosu-ro, Ilsandong-gu, Goyang-si, Gyeonggi-do
경기도 고양시 일산동구 호수로 731

Onemount 원마운트

Onemount is a huge entertainment complex near KINTEX and Ilsan Lake Park. Onemount itself contains three buildings with a shopping mall, event spaces, luxury sports club, a theme park and the snow park. The Onemount Snowpark is an indoor winter theme park, the first one created in South Korea. It offers an ice lake to skate on, both indoor and outdoor sledding, restaurants and photo opportunities. The Onemount Water Park has both indoor and outdoor attractions including a wave pool, water slides, and various rides. BTS came to Onemount to film Episodes 13-16 of Run BTS!

In episodes 13 and 14 of Run BTS the members introduce the Onemount Water Park and discuss that it is in RM's hometown. In these episodes SUGA is the MC and the others divide themselves into two teams: younger and older. They are competing to select meals at the end of the show but the catch is there's a spy among them and if they do not guess correctly who it is then they will have to watch the spy eat all their food. For all of episode 13 the members are in the indoor water park in an area known as the 'carnival beach.' Here they race through roller balls, wrestle against each other on floating platforms and try a (hilarious) obstacle course. Other attractions featured in the show include the Kingball ride, the Fantastic Flex pool, the Tugel Ride and the Sky Boomerango which served as punishment for the losers.

Episode 16 is set at the Onemount Snow Park and the theme of the episode is 'BTS Winter Olympic Games.' BTS started the game in the outdoor sledding area known as 'Everslide' to race in tube sleds and capture flags. The next round moves to the indoor ice rink for a game of curling and the most hilarious version of sled racing you could imagine. Whether it was the cold air, being on ice, or the adrenalin of sleddings, all seven members seem extra energetic and giggly in this episode which is a ringing endorsement for One-mount Snow Park.

Onemount is open all year round, opening 10am each day and closing either 6pm weekdays or 7pm on weekends. You can purchase all day tickets onsite. You can also rent equipment inside such as a life vest, sunbed, beach chair or tent for an additional cost. The same is possible for renting skates and sleds from the snow park during the winter months.

For updates on the parks and their operations you can check their website: www.onemount.co.kr

300, Hallyu world-ro, Ilsanseo-gu, Goyang-si, Gyeonggi-do
경기도 고양시 일산서구 한류월드로 300

Hugok Academy Village 후곡마을학원

"Hugok Hagwon Village that raised me in my young years" - Ma City

RM studied very hard when he was young and was a very good student. He attended many hagwons in Ilsan, all of them located in the 'academy village' in the town of Hugok. This area is basically one long street of tall buildings packed with academies for every subject you can think of: English, math, essay writing, piano, etc. If you walk down this street you will also notice many yellow shuttle buses: these are designated for carrying students to and from their academies. RM would have used these almost daily. It's not a good idea to go inside these buildings, but walking along them and marveling at the study culture that exists in Ilsan, and Korea in general, will give you some insight into what it was like growing up here for RM.

576, Ilsan-ro, Ilsanseo-gu, Goyang-si, Gyeonggi-do
경기도 고양시 일산서구 일산로 576

Sinil Middle School 신일중학교

While we do know the schools that each BTS member attended, not all of them advertise this fact. Sinil Middle School is the only school out of the four RM attended in Ilsan that has anything related to BTS on display - here it is a small plaque indicating that there is a private 'RM Forest' inside the school. It is illegal to enter the school, but you can easily walk by as it's a short distance from the Hugok Academy Village.

177, Gobong-ro, Ilsanseo-gu, Goyang-si, Gyeonggi-do
경기도 고양시 일산서구 고봉로 177

Day Trip

Gunsan

———

Wolmyeong Park

Gunsan Medical Center

Eunpa Reservoir

1 OT7 Mural - Jigok Elementary School

2 Jin Mural

3 Jimin and Jin Mural

4 Jimin Mural

5 j-hope Mural

6 SUGA Mural

7 Jungkook Mural and V Mural

Gunsan
군산

Gunsan is a port city in the north of Jeollabuk-do, or North Jeolla Province. It's an industrial city on the south bank of the Geum river and is rich with history. The city originally was a fishing village, but during the Japanese occupation it became a port city to grow and transport rice to Japan. Gunsan was left relatively untouched during the Korean War and has remnant historical pieces tied to the Japanese occupation, including the only Japanese Buddhist style temple left in Korea. The Gunsan Islands surround Gunsan, the most popular of which is Seonyudo Island (선유도) which you can get to by ferry.

At first Gunsan does not appear to have any connection to BTS, but there is something unique about Gunsan these days. Not only is the filming site for BTS's music video "Save Me" in an area just outside of Gunsan, but nowadays there are BTS murals dotted across the town. This is thanks to local graffiti artist Lee Jongbae, who goes by the artist name 'Staz.' He has been a muralist since 1999, grew up in Gunsan, and is a BTS fan. Since both BTS and ARMY have been spreading Korean culture internationally, he wanted to say thanks by doing what he does best: street art murals. Though he started in Gunsan, he now has

Gunsan

Gunsan station

completed projects all around South Korea and has started doing some in the US as well. Tracking them all down with their addresses is a little bit like doing an intense treasure hunt where you have to figure out the clues yourself, but here's a starting list for the Gunsan BTS murals!

How to get to Gunsan

KTX

You can travel to Gunsan by the KTX through the Iksan Station train line. This means you will first travel from Seoul Station to Iksan Station (a trip that takes roughly 1.5 hours) and then another short 20 minute train from Iksan Station to Gunsan Station. Trains for Iksan depart hourly from Seoul Station. You should allow up to 2.5 hours for this trip and prices range between 28,000 KRW and 32,000 KRW. You can purchase the tickets online through the Korean rail website or in person at the train station.

Intercity Express Bus

This Express bus is the most direct route to Gunsan and is the most comfortable. You will depart from Seoul Central City Bus Terminal located in Gangnam and be driven directly to the Gunsan Intercity Bus Terminal, with one rest stop in the middle. Buses leave from Seoul to Gunsan every 30 minutes and the journey takes 2.5 hours. Tickets cost between 13,000 KRW and 21,000 KRW.

Getting around Gunsan

If you are not using a car, then public buses are your best option for venturing across Gunsan. However, unlike the big cities, Gunsan's public transport system runs more like a small town, which can mean one bus every hour. Don't be surprised that upon missing your bus you end up waiting an extended period of time for the next one. Gunsan is a very walkable city though and many of the murals are a 20 minute walk from each other. If you get stuck you can catch taxis very easily here too, and while more expensive than the bus, are not too hard on the wallet.

The Murals

These murals are scattered around Gunsan, with the majority of them within a 20 minute bus ride of the city center. Rather than provide an exact order to see them, you can enter the locations in your map of choice and design your own route.

OT7 Mural - Jigok Elementary School 지곡초등학교

This is a beautiful mural of all seven members that decorates 60 meters of the elementary school's outer brick walls. This is a newer addition to Staz's collection and the likenesses of each member are truly impressive. The mural

Mural - Jigok Elementary School

Jimin and Jin Mural

is on the road between the school and the Gunsan Girls' Commercial High School. It's fun to get up close and notice all the intricate details of the street art, but to really get the best impact you are better off crossing the road and looking from a bit more distance. It's a short ride from the Gunsan Intercity Bus station or the city center.

26 Sinji-gil, Gunsan-si, Jeollabuk-do
전라북도 군산시 신지길 26

Jin Mural

Slightly further away from the previously mentioned mural is one dedicated to Jin. This area is on the other side of the Mije Reservoir (one of three in Gunsan) and the campus for Gunsan National University. Similar to the layout of the OT7 mural at Jigok Elementary School, the Jin mural stretches along a pathway on the corner of Yongmun Elementary School. But rather than brick, this mural is on sheet metal, similar to the material that is used for corrugated roofing. This mural depicts the "Butter" era Jin in shades of black, white and gray, with patches of purple behind him and the word 'HOPE' spelled next to him similarly in bright colors.

32 Miryong-ro, Gunsan-si, Jeollabuk-do
전라북도 군산시 미룡로 32

Jimin and Jin Mural

Within walking distance from the OT7 mural is this one of Jin and Jimin, also from the "Butter" era. Jimin in particular stands out with his rainbow hair and oversized sunglasses but Staz made sure to do Jin's stunning facial features justice too. Like all the individual murals, it's in a random and innocuous location. This mural is on a corner with a cafe, stores and an empty building lot around it. The area is actually something of a main street with businesses, clothing stores, cafés and restaurants lined up on both sides of the road. If you like to browse, whether it's the main chains or independent stores, then this is the place for you.

206 Wolmyeong-ro, Gunsan-si, Jeollabuk-do
전라북도 군산시 월명로 206

Jimin Mural

This Jimin mural is basically a floating piece of street art as it's snuggled in-between a gym and a random workshop on a side street. It's less than a five minute walk from the above mentioned Jin and Jimin mural. This mural depicts blonde-and-pink-haired Jimin and seems to be from the "Boy With Luv" era, especially as he is holding a rose, but the lyrics surrounding him are from

"Butter." It is wonderful that this mural makes you go down various side streets, drawing you away from the temptations of the main street. There are various smaller cafes around this mural, so this might be the perfect time to grab a refreshing drink or snack.

29 Chukdongan 3-gil, Gunsan-si, Jeollabuk-do
전라북도 군산시 축동안3길 29

j-hope Mural

This one is extra fun to find as it's tucked away in a corner you'd never know was there unless made to look, which is rather the beauty of street art. This j-hope is in black and white and shows the sunshine member of the group in a black open-

Jimin Mural

collared shirt, oozing confidence with his signature charming smile. The mural is at the Gunsan Beer Port, right on the water. If you are facing towards the water you want to head to the right handside of the beer port building, otherwise you'll walk around the entire building to find this one. The stunning visual of j-hope is at the entrance of a staircase that leads to a great open air rooftop with views out over the port. It's a very quiet area with not a lot of activity, which makes it extra nice to stroll around here. If you come while the tide is out you will see the amazing spectacle of how far the water recedes. As you'd expect, most of the restaurants and stores in the area specialize in seafood and fishing: don't be alarmed if you see various sea creatures drying out in the sun.

146-24 Haemang-ro, Gunsan-si, Jeollabuk-do
전라북도 군산시 해망로 146-24

SUGA Mural

A street back from his bandmate j-hope's mural, is one dedicated to SUGA. It's at the dead-end of the street and has been turned into a simple garden area with some benches and flowers around it. The portrait is a side profile and depicts a blonde SUGA with his iconic smile and nose scrunch. Compared to j-hope's mural around the corner that used a mostly black and white palette, this one of SUGA includes a green outfit and vibrant blue background with butterflies and flowers. This mural takes up the whole of the building and is a very cute place to take a photo.

Not far from here is the Gunsan Modern Art Museum, Gunsan Modern History Museum and the Jinpo Maritime Theme Park. The latter especially is fun as there are vintage warships, aircrafts and tanks that you can get up close to and even enter some of them. The exhibition hall includes more information about Gunsan's maritime history. This all with the backdrop of the port and Dongbaek Bridge makes for a few fun hours of exploring. If you want to get a ticket to enter the Modern History Museum and

j-hope Mural

SUGA Mural

the Wingbongham warship, you can get an integrated admission ticket that will allow entry for both from the Modern History museum. This ticket will include access to the Bank of Joseon and the Modern Architecture Museum as well.

. . . .

Note: Some of the museums are not accessible in English, so prepare to use your translation app.

146-49 Haemang-ro, Gunsan-si, Jeollabuk-do
전라북도 군산시 해망로 146-49

Jung Kook Mural - Gyeongamdong Railroad Village 경암동 철길마을

In another area of Gunsan is possibly the city's most famous and unique tourist destination: the Gyeongamdong Railroad Village (철길마을). What were once disused railroads left by the Japanese have now turned into an open air city attraction designed to transport visitors back in time. The stores here all sell either candy, toys or various items from the post-Korean war era. A lot of Koreans come here to reminisce or share with their younger family members things they grew up with in the 50s, 60s and 70s. One unique activity here is renting out older school uniforms from the 70s and 80s and having your own photoshoots. This makes the Railroad Village a popular spot for couples and young families.

There is an abundance of street art in this Railroad Village, including a mural dedicated to BTS's youngest member,

Jungkook Mural

Jung Kook. Most of the stores center around the old railroads, but running parallel to this is a regular street where you can find a red model train. Behind this train, on the wall of the cafe, is Jung Kook's mural! This version of Jung Kook is from the vocal line's famous performance of "Dimple," where he is wearing a flowy spotted shirt and has longer hair. Staz the artist paid great attention to his facial expression in this painting as his gaze looks especially dreamy.

Note: If you research online you might find that this Railroad Village also had a mural dedicated to V where he was split into 'angel' and 'devil'. This used to be on a brick wall of a restaurant, but has since been covered over. While disappointing, it doesn't take away from how enjoyable the Railroad Village and Jung Kook murals are to visit.

49 Gyeongchonan 3-gil, Gunsan-si, Jeollabuk-do
전라북도 군산시 경촌안3길 49

V Mural

Further out in Gunsan, past the Gunsan airport, is a random gas station with a small CU store covered in street art. Possibly the largest mural includes that of blue-haired V. This is one of the first mural art pieces Staz the artist ever created, since he is a V bias. This one is extra special because he also included Yeontan ('Tan' for short), V's pomeranian dog, on the side of the container as well. Keep in mind that this mural is a 50 minute bus ride out of town and so might be worth doing earlier in your list or risk running out of time otherwise. If you have access to a car or taxi then it is a more manageable 15 minute car ride.

534-5 Saemangeumbuk-ro, Gunsan-si, Jeollabuk-do
전라북도 군산시 새만금북로 534-5

RM Mural - Munyeon 2-Gu Bus Cafe
무녀2구 버스카페

This spot is most out of the way of all the known murals in Gunsan and best accessed by car or taxi. It's a spot where many of the islands in the area are connected by walking paths. The area is a popular spot for hikers as there are a lot of trails and islands to explore. The Munyeon 2-Gu Bus Cafe is on Munyeo Island. This is a cafe that in its yard has a collection of buses, ranging from double decker to classic yellow school bus, all of which you can climb inside. Some are even converted into extra seating for the cafe. Although it is a cafe, this place is best known for its burgers, and the RM mural that exists here too. This particular mural has a silver-haired RM with his dimple on full display next to his BT21 creation, Koya. There is a message on this one, unlike all the others, that reads '28th Happy Namjoon Day' as this was a birthday project done for RM's 28th birthday in 2021, much like the one in his hometown, Ilsan.

To get here by public transport requires two buses and over an hour and half travel time from the center of Gunsan. If you decide to catch a taxi or have access to a car then it's a 45 minute drive.

Note: This is somewhat on the way to the filming location for BTS's "Save Me" Music Video if you have access to a car.

Munyeon 2-Gu Bus Cafe is open everyday 9:00am-7:00pm

San 10-14 Munyeodo-ri, Okdo-myeon, Gunsan-si, Jeollabuk-do
전라북도 군산시 옥도면 무녀도리 산10-14

Save Me MV filming location

In 2016, BTS released their music video for "Save Me" which was a one-shot choreography piece filmed on what looked like a stormy beach. This was actually in an area outside Gunsan known as Saemangeum inside the Byeonsan district, now somewhat known for its Saemangeum seawall that connects the Buan county to Gunsan. It's essentially reclaimed land that is being redeveloped into a new port and business area. To find the area you will need to search for 'Saemangeum Project Office' into your navigation system of choice. From there you will drive towards 'Haechang Dock' before walking a path by foot to the patch of land. The ongoing work in the area means it is not guaranteed to look exactly like the scene from the music video, or be that easy to find, but it would be a fun time practicing the choreo here for yourself since there is unlikely to be anyone other than you there or other ARMY.

1044-53 Baengnyeon-ri Haseo-myeon Buan-gun Jeollabuk-do
전라북도 부안군 하서면 백련리 1044-53

BAIDU SUGA BA

Youth Arts and Culture Street

Day Trip

Daegu

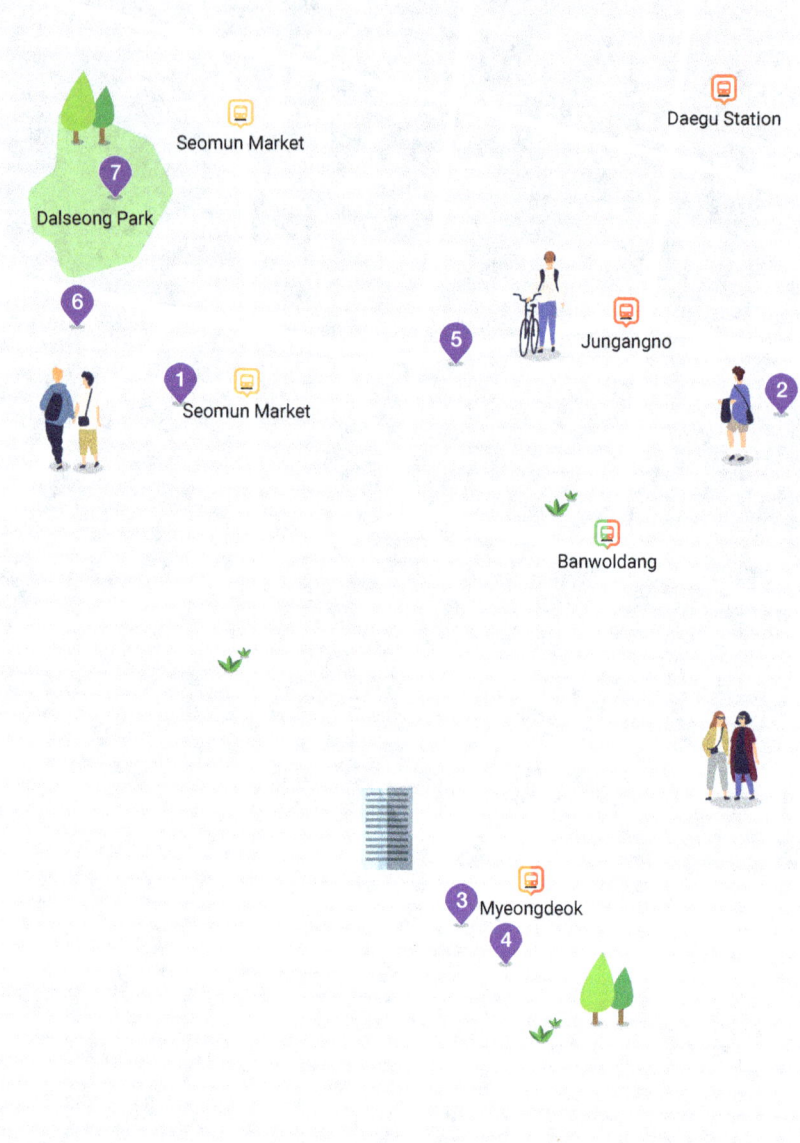

1. Seomun Market
2. ferris wheel in Sparkland
3. Youth Arts and Culture Street
4. Namsan-dong Music Street
5. BAS Academy
6. Daeseong Elementary School
7. Dalseong Park

Daegu
대구

Daegu is in the south-east of the Korean peninsula in the Gyeongsang province, and is Korea's third largest metropolitan city after Seoul and Busan. It is an eco-conscious city, with one of three global climate clocks located here. Daegu has maintained a youth culture, which can be rare outside of Seoul, and so has a thriving art and cafe scene, making it a great day trip to relax and enjoy time away from the bigger city vibes. Popular destinations in Daegu include the Seomun Market (서문시장), the street dedicated to famous singer and musician Kim Kwang-seok (김광석다시그리기길), or the ferris wheel in Sparkland (스파크랜드): a theme park located on top of a building. Daegu also has a wide range of beautiful parks, mountains and temples if you want to get away from the bustle of crowds for a while.

Daegu is the hometown of members SUGA and V. SUGA talks about his upbringing in Daegu often in his music, especially in his solo work as Agust D. The moniker 'Agust D' is a recognition of his roots, as 'Agust D' is 'Dt SUGA' backwards, where the 'DT' stands for Daegu Town. This significance, in addition to the various locations we share here, make Daegu a strong recommendation when traveling to Korea.

Dongdaegu Station

How to get to Daegu

There are various methods of getting to Daegu from Seoul, but for a day trip the main options are either KTX or Intercity Express bus.

KTX Train

You can take a KTX train from Seoul Station to Dongdaegu station and arrive in just over 90 minutes. There are multiple trains departing every hour, but it is still wise to book a ticket ahead of time. Tickets can be purchased either online through the Korean rail website (https://www.letskorail.com/ebizbf/EbizbfForeign_pr16100.do?gubun=1), or in person at the station. A roundtrip ticket will cost around 70,000 KRW but this can vary depending on the day and time you select, as well as if you get a first or second class seat.

Intercity Express Bus

If you want a more cost-effective but comfortable method of traveling to Daegu, then the Intercity Express bus is an option. Though take note that it is a four hour journey from Seoul without traffic, so not the most ideal for a short term trip. The bus will depart from either Seoul Gyeongbu Express Bus Terminal or Dongseoul Bus Terminal.

You can purchase your ticket on the departure date at the ticket counter.

ferris wheel in Sparkland

There are also two options to choose from: 'Economy,' which is a regular bus with four seats in each row, or 'Excellent,' which is a bus with larger seats and only three seats in each row. For a one-way ticket in the 'Economy' class, the estimated cost would be around 19,000 KRW, and in the 'Excellent' class the ticket price would be around 27,400 KRW.

If you prefer booking your ticket online, you can do that here: https://txbuse.t-money.co.kr/ or here https://www.kobus.co.kr/mrs/satschc.do

Prices and schedule times may vary according to time, day and season.

From Busan

A great option is to take a day trip to Daegu from Busan, as the train ride is 40 minutes and runs multiple times an hour. You depart from Busan Station and arrive at Dongdaegu Station. You can expect a roundtrip ticket to cost between 20,000-30,000 KRW and can be purchased at the station on the day or online at the Korean rail website.

Getting around Daegu

Daegu has convenient and reliable public transport, making traveling around easy. It has three train lines, one of which is an above ground monorail system (line 3).

Daegu Bus

All stations are announced in Korean and English at least, making navigation very simple. The buses are also frequent and have many routes, meaning it is usually easy and not too time-consuming getting from one area of town to another. The bus stops are clearly marked with lists of the buses that stop there and the announcements on the bus for each stop are usually done in Korean and English. Using a navigation app such as Naver Maps or Kakao Maps will make getting around Daegu with public transport effortless and efficient.

Youth Arts and Culture Street
청년예술문화거리

In an area known as the 'Youth Arts and Culture Street' are a collection of

Youth Arts and Culture Street

murals dedicated to SUGA. The easiest way to navigate this area is to head to Myeongdeok Station (Line 1 or 3) and use exit 3. In front of you will be a small side street that will take you almost directly to a 7-Eleven with the first Yoongi art display. It's a cute animated version of Agust D from his "Daechwita" music video. As you continue down the street you will also pass a small parking area with a pink mural with SUGA-letter graffiti. Make sure you check the other side of the road because next to the Mul Begi Korean Table restaurant (물베기한정식) on the side of a building is a large SUGA mural in yellow with a list of his popular songs such as "So Far Away," "Daechwita," "Seesaw," "Eight," "That That" and other works he has produced. Even though it's large, it can be easy to miss as you walk further down the street with your back to it.

In front of the House of Youth Culture (청년문화의집) is another series of SUGA murals. The murals extend around a corner, and one section is often used as a parking area so it can be hard to see them properly. There are four murals in this section, one of which depicts SUGA from the "Permission to Dance" music video; this version is wearing denim and laying down next to a cassette that reads "Butter." In total there are four versions of Yoongi and the murals are very bright and punchy, mainly using primary colors.

Around the corner in a different section is a more muted version of a SUGA mural, featuring a blonde Yoongi from his "Agust D" music video and another with him wearing a suit next to the lyrics from "So Far Away." Considering the House of Youth Culture street is to inspire young artists, the lyrics chosen from the song focusing on dreams seems very poignant and deliberate: "Dream, may your creation be with you at the end of your life. Dream, that it will be generous no matter where you are." This area is right next to Namsan-dong music street, where SUGA used to work in a studio and is often referencing in his lyrics. SUGA worked hard in this area and sacrificed a lot to follow, and eventually achieve, his dreams. This is a beautiful recognition of both his past and his accomplishments.

23, Jungang-daero 51gil, Nam-gu, Daegu
대구 남구 중앙대로 51길 23
Myeongdeok Station 명덕역, Exit 3 (Daegu line 1, 3)

1801-1, Daemyeong-dong, Nam-gu, Daegu 대구 남구 대명동 1801-1
Myeongdeok Station 명덕역, Exit 3 (Daegu line 1, 3)

60, Jungang-daero 51gil, Nam-gu, Daegu
대구 남구 중앙대로 51길 60
Myeongdeok Station 명덕역, Exit 3 (Daegu line 1, 3)

Namsan-dong Music Street
남산동 악기거리

"From a basement studio in Namsan-dong to Apgujeong, I laid my beat, the origin of my youth" - Intro: Never Mind

Namsan-dong Instrument Street is a place centered around music with an abundance of instrument stores and music practice rooms everywhere. This is one of the locations where SUGA used to work and study music, though it wasn't always a positive experience. SUGA has said that he often was not paid for his work and if he overspent on a meal here (paying 1,500 KRW instead of 1,000 KRW for noodles) he would not be able to pay for a bus fare and instead spend 3 hours walking home. It obviously left an impact on him as he mentions his time in Namsan-dong in various songs ("Intro: Never Mind," "Hip Hop Phile," "Moonlight" etc.) and therefore makes walking around this area, which is around the corner from the mural street, a worthwhile experience. Plus, this is another area full of installation art, making turning every corner potentially a fun surprise.

1792-1, Daemyeong-dong, Nam-gu, Daegu 대구 남구 대명동 1792-1
Myeongdeok Station 명덕역, Exit 4 (Daegu line 1, 3)

BAS Academy 바스아카데미

This is the music academy that SUGA was attending when he went to audition for BigHit's 'Hit It!' rap competition. He would

BAS Academy

BAS Academy

ride the 724 bus from his high school (Kangbok High School 강복고등학교) to this studio to work, which would take up to an hour. He wrote a song about his time traveling to this studio, how he pushed for his dreams, comparing it with his efforts in Seoul too, and named the song after the two bus routes: "724148." The bus still operates outside this academy today. The academy allows you to go in and see posters that celebrate their artists, including SUGA. But as this place is still active for teaching, you cannot go up the stairs and tour around. The building is very easily identifiable as it is a bright orange and on one side has a giant photo printed of SUGA. There are also a lot of cafés in this area, perfect for taking a break and thinking about a

teenage version of SUGA walking to and from this area everyday years ago.

530, Gukchaebosang-ro, Jung-gu, Daegu
대구 중구 하서동 8-2
Jungangno Station 중앙로역, Exit 1
(Daegu line 1)

Daeseong Elementary School
대성초등학교

This elementary school is one V attended before he moved away to live with his grandparents. What makes this school significant is that as a birthday project in 2021, fans decided to have a mural celebrating V and his solo works made on the outer wall of the school. It is 33 meters wide and 2 meters tall and uses one of V's favorite art pieces, Van Gogh's 'Starry Night' as a background. In various languages are messages of 'We Purple U' and 'Taehyung, I love you' stretched across the wall. It also has the images of 11 of V's solo songs, projects, and photos he has shared over the years. It's a beautiful area to walk around and is out of the way enough that it does not interfere with the school, meaning you can take your time appreciating the art installation. Upon arriving here, you will find that a small street market is set up daily in front of the wall too, which makes for a lively atmosphere.

Daeseong Elementary School

426, Gukchaebosang-ro, Bisan 4(sa)-dong, Seo-gu, Daegu 대구 서구 비산4동 국채보상로 426 Seomun Market Station 서문시장역, Exit 2 (Daegu line 3)

Dalseong Park 달성공원

This is a deceptively large park that is a block over from the Daeseong Elementary School featuring V's mural. This park used to be the sight of a fortress, as Daegu was once its own kingdom, but now it has beautiful walking paths, gardens, monuments and a very random zoo. This park is special to V as he used to come here as a child with his family. He has even shared a photo of his toddler self running around in front a tree in this park, and then shared him recreating that photo again in 2015, running in the same manner and position. Since then this tree has become a bit of an icon for ARMY. You cannot walk on the grass area where V stood (you require special permission) but the tree is still very photographic. V also shared selfies in front of the monkeys and elephants at the zoo here too. This is a really nice spot to slow down for a moment and appreciate this patch of nature in the middle of a city. It's especially remarkable that you can see historical elements like the pavilion gates or monuments with the backdrop of tall city buildings: a duality that is quite prominent in Korea.

35, Dalseonggongwon-ro, Dalseong-dong, Jung-gu, Daegu 대구 중구 달성공원로 35 Dalseong Park Station 달성공원역, Exit 3 (Daegu line 3)

Dalseong Park

Maengbang Beach

Weekend Trip

Gangneung

——

1 Gangneung station

2 Haslla Art World

3 Neungpadae

4 Samyang Ranch

5 BTS bus stop

6 Jumunjin Fish Market

7 Maengbang Beach

Gangneung
강릉

A weekend away in Gangneung

Practical information

For people living in Seoul, Gangneung is a popular place for a weekend getaway because it's not too far away. Roughly two hours by train from Seoul, Gangneung is on South Korea's east coast. You can find many beaches along the coast, while the downtown area features historical landmarks, museums and other fun things to discover. The beautiful forest trails, filled with the scent of pine, are a wonderful break from bustling city life. Combining beautiful nature with the city has never been more charming.

Let's talk about how to get to Gangneung.

KTX train

You can travel from Seoul to Gangneung by taking the KTX high-speed train. With train intervals of 1 hour, you can easily plan your departure and arrival according to your schedule. The journey time is around 2 hours and covers a distance of 222km. The fastest train takes 1h 50min.

A return ticket from Seoul to Gangneung costs you around 89,000 KRW, but keep in mind that prices depend on when

Gangneung

you're traveling. Prices are usually higher on weekends. You can purchase your train tickets up to one month in advance.

Tickets can be purchased either online through the Korean rail website (https://www.letskorail.com/ebizbf/EbizbfForeign_pr16100.do?gubun=1), or in person at the train station.

KTX trains from Seoul to Gangneung depart from Seoul Station and arrive at Gangneung station.

Intercity Express bus

Another comfortable way to get to Gangneung from Seoul is to use the Intercity Express bus departing from Seoul Gyeongbu Express Bus Terminal (Gangnam) and Dongseoul Bus Terminal. Both stations are easily accessible by subway. The estimated duration of the journey is around 2h20min. The Intercity Express buses will bring you from Seoul to Gangneung every 30 minutes.

You can purchase your ticket on the departure date at the ticket counter. You can choose between an 'Economy' seat or 'Excellent' seat. For a return ticket in the "Economy" class, you can expect the price to be around 30,000 KRW and in the "Excellent" class, the ticket price may go up to 42,000 KRW.

If you prefer booking your ticket online, you can do that here: https://txbuse.t-money.co.kr/ or here https://www.kobus.co.kr/mrs/satschc.do

Getting around Gangneung

The city center is easy to navigate on foot. For any destination outside the city center, you can get around by bus or taxi. Gangneung's public transport system is very convenient to use since it connects the different areas of the city. Unfortunately, unlike Seoul or Busan, the information about bus stops etc, are not provided in any other language than Korean, so make sure to memorize the Korean/Hangul version of your bus stop. Also, some buses may not have arrival times available on the navigation apps. For the following itinerary, it is worth a rental car, or prepare to take a taxi.

Saturday in Gangneung

Saturday morning: Haslla Art World

In order to have an unforgettable experience in Gangneung, you shouldn't miss the Haslla Art World museum. The secluded place offers an incredible view of the ocean but is known for its fantastic art museum divided into three sections: the Modern Art Museum, the Pinocchio Museum and the Outdoor Museum. There's something to see wherever you look. Get ready to be hypnotized by the other worldliness of Haslla Art World.

Haslla Art World

1 pm: Neungpadae (능파대) BTS's winter for every season

Neungpadae served as a shooting location for the 2021 Winter Package. Finding the exact spot can be challenging since the area looks very similar with its impressive rocks and crashing waves. On your way back you could make a stop in Sokcho (속초), a popular getaway spot that is located nearby Seoraksan national park (설악산공원).

Alternatively, if you prefer taking a peaceful walk in quiet green scenery, you can also visit Daegwallyeong Samyang Ranch (대관령삼양목장). Adding character to the area are its wind turbines and the tranquil walking trails. Similar to the previous location, it may be a bit difficult to find the exact spot where BTS did their photoshoot, but it never hurts to try!

Sunday in Gangneung

Sunday morning: Rise and shine and BTS bus stop

This is arguably the most popular destination for ARMY in Gangneung is the cover for BTS's album You Never Walk Alone (2017) which featured this bus stop at Jumunjin Beach (주문진해변). You can find the BTS bus stop under 'BTS 버스정류장 (bus stop)' in the navigation apps, and there are posted signs at Jumunjin Beach that indicate the way. BTS also filmed parts of the "Spring Day" music video at Jumunjin too.

Neungpadae

Neungpadae

Jumunjin Beach is located in the northernmost part of the city. There are a variety of amenities along the beach, like restaurants facing the beach, a fitness park and much more. Some of the restaurants require you to order through

BTS bus stop

the Naver app, so if you don't have a Naver account and are unfamiliar with Korean, you may have to ask nicely to get your burger. Therefore it might be better to have your meal before or after you visit the bus stop. As Gangneung is near the sea, it is most famous for its fresh seafood. The sheer variety and reasonable price tag may make you feel like you've hit the gourmet jackpot. If you are like Namjoon and do not like seafood, there is no need to worry! You will find plenty of other delicious options. A unique point of the beach is the surrounding pine trees that offer shade during sunny beach days. The shallow and clear sea makes this beach a highlight for many tourists.

Gangneung is also well known for offering various places to watch the sunrise. So you might want to consider watching the sunrise at Jumunjin Beach.

#Photoshoot, #MusicVideo

12 pm: Fish market for seafood lovers

Jumunjin Fish Market is an exciting place to explore traditional Korean food in Gangneung. Currently operated by about 70 merchants, Jumunjin Fish Market is the largest seafood market on the east coast. It specializes in seafood caught on the east coast such as squid, mackerel,

pollacks etc. Another highlight of this place is a sashimi center where seafood lovers can enjoy some fresh seafood.

For those that don't like seafood, but still want to have the food market experience, there is Jungang Market. This is where you can get Gangneung specialties, like spicy fried chicken. With Gangneung being a coastal city, fresh seafood is inevitable, but you can find other options at Jungang Market.

1 pm: Maengbang Beach (맹방해수욕장), Smooth like ... Samcheok?

Driving one and a half hours by car (mostly highway) will lead you to Maengbang Beach in Samcheok. Many of you will

Maengbang Beach

Maengbang Beach

recognize the beach setting of the "Butter Jacket Shooting." Several BTS signs and banners will make it obvious that you have reached the "Butter" album jacket shooting spot.

The narrow but long beach leads to a beautiful island that gives you the opportunity to stroll around and relax a bit. The first eye-catcher will be the huge "Permission to Dance" inspired BTS sign that lights up in the dark. Right next to this sign are the deckchairs. The deck chairs are for the public, so many people sunbathe there. Next to the deck chairs, you can find the high seat on which the members also took pictures for the "Butter" album. The whole beach, with its chairs, high seat, volleyball, and surfboards, offers

great photo opportunities to recreate the "Butter" photoshoot.

Note: Make sure to have a meal before getting there since there are no restaurants in the vicinity.

Free parking is available on the opposite of the beach.

Insider tip: Make sure to visit this place before 5 pm before the staff closes all of the umbrellas.

On your way to Maengbang Beach, make sure to take the Haean-ro, which leads you along the sea and gives you beautiful sights that you'll remember forever.

Gwangalli Beach

Weekend Trip

Busan

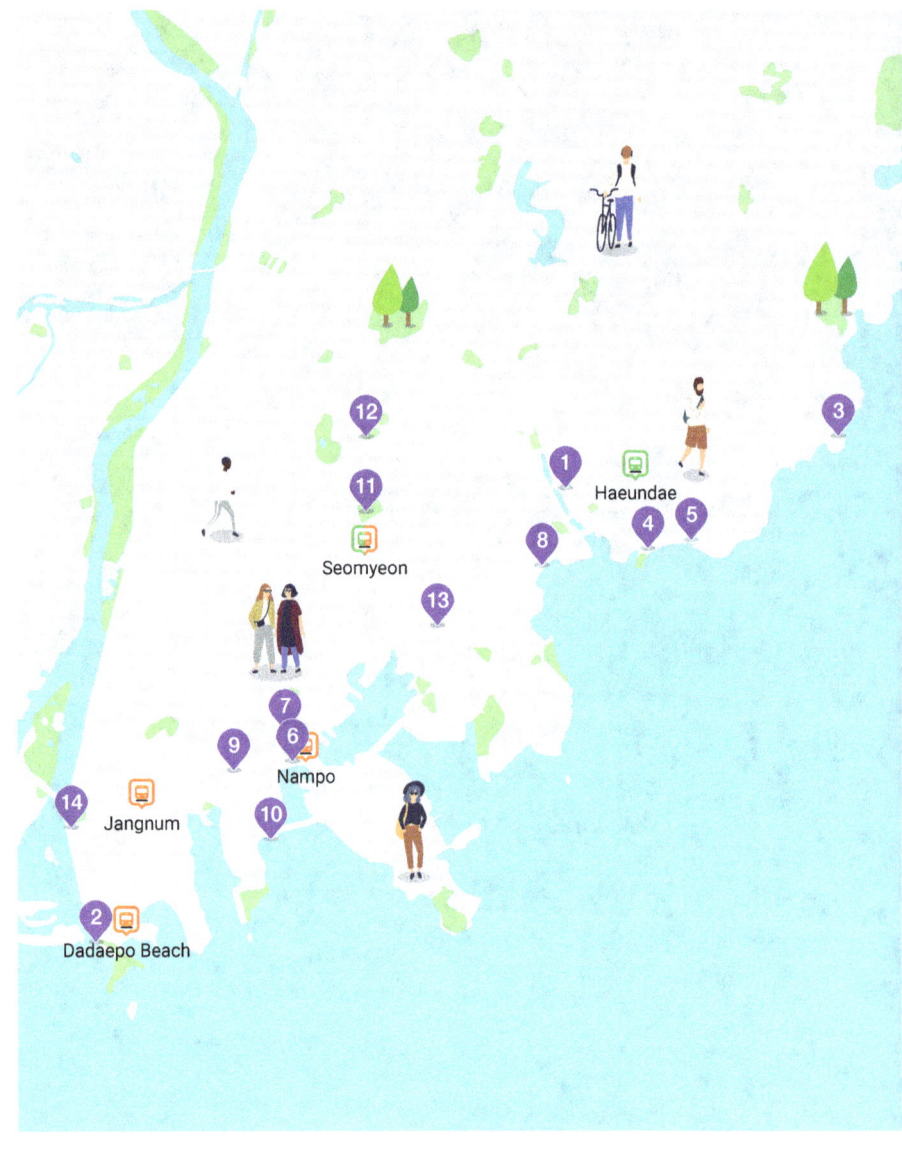

1. DAH museum
2. Dadaepo Beach
3. Yonggungsa Temple
4. Haeundae
5. Sky Capsule
6. Jagalchi Market
7. Gukje market
8. Gwangalli beach
9. Gamcheon Culture Village
10. Song Marine Cable Car
11. Busan Citizen Park
12. Busan Asiad Auxiliary Stadium
13. Magnate Café
14. Jangnim Port

Busan
부산

*"Hey, the sea of busan
...Under the blue sky, this skyline
... Come to ma city" -Ma City, The Most
Beautiful Moment In Life: Young Forever*

Located at the southeastern tip of the Korean peninsula, Busan is the second largest city in Korea. Besides being famous for its beaches, temples and mountains, it is also well known among ARMY for being the hometown of members Jimin and Jung Kook.

In October 2022, the city of Busan turned purple to celebrate their free concert BTS Yet To Come in Busan on October 15th. The concert was to support South Korea's bid to host the World Expo 2030 in Busan, for which BTS were made official ambassadors earlier in July 2022. The event, which took place a couple of months after Korea lifted their travel restrictions for foreigners, attracted ARMY from all over Korea and the world. In celebration of the event, Busan's airport, Gimhae International Airport, turned purple to greet ARMY arriving in the city for the show. The bridge at Gwangalli Beach, one of the most popular beaches in Busan, also turned purple in honor

of BTS. Multiple hotels, such as Grand Josun, Paradise, Lotte, Marriott, and Park Hyatt, offered BTS goodies for the fans to enjoy during their stay. Paradise Hotel even decorated the area outside with a bunch of BTS-themed stuff. The goodies provided by each hotel included towels, slippers, photocards, shower supplies, bags, etc. There were live viewings of the concert across the city for those unable to get tickets for the show. Simultaneously with the concert, the "2022 BTS Exhibition: the Proof in Busan" was held from October 5th, 2022, until November 8th, 2022. You could say that the city truly turned into a purple BTS paradise for ARMY to enjoy in every way possible.

If you are looking for the perfect weekend getaway, you should definitely consider Busan. It offers an extensive range of breathtaking sights and a variety of activities for everyone. The coastal town and its beaches, mountains, fish markets, and animated nightlife make Busan worth its while.

Practical information

There are a few different ways to get to Busan depending on time and budget.

KTX train

The easiest and most popular way to travel from Seoul to Busan is on the KTX

Busan Station

high-speed train. There are also slower trains like the ITX, but the KTX is probably the most convenient one.

KTX is a network of high-speed trains that extends throughout the whole country. The direct trains depart hourly and take you from Seoul to Busan in under three hours, which is fast considering the distance between the two cities is 329km (approx. 204 miles).

In general, a return ticket from Seoul to Busan, Busan to Seoul is about 120,000 KRW, but prices are subject to change depending on your travel date and time. Tickets are cheaper on weekdays during off-peak times. You can expect higher prices on weekends.

Tickets can be purchased either online through the Korean rail website (https://www.letskorail.com/ebizbf/EbizbfForeign_pr16100.do?gubun=1), or in person at the station. You can purchase them from the vending machines or at the ticket counters. Technically you could be spontaneous, but keep in mind that tickets might sell out during weekends and bank holidays, so be sure to plan your trip accordingly.

KTX trains from Seoul to Busan depart both at Seoul Station and at Yongsan Station. Both stations are easily accessible by subway and bus.

Source: https://www.letskorail.com/ebizbf/EbizbfForeign_pr16100.do?gubun=1

ITX, SRT, Mugunghwa

If you are not bound by time and looking for a more affordable way to get from Seoul to Busan, you might want to consider ITX, SRT or Mugunghwa trains. These trains are not as fast as the KTX, but they are more affordable. The length of the journey and prices depend on which train you choose. But it is safe to say that the longer the journey, the cheaper the ticket.

The process for purchasing slow train tickets is exactly the same as purchasing KTX tickets. You can purchase your tickets online through the Korean Railway website or in person at any train station. Keep in mind that they run less frequently than the KTX train does, so you have fewer departure times to choose from.

When it comes to departure locations from Seoul to Busan, it depends on the type of train you will be taking. The ITX trains depart from either Seoul Station or Yeongdeungpo Station, which is located south across the river, not too far from Gimpo Airport.

The SRT train, which is the quickest among the slower trains and takes about as long as a KTX, only departs from Suseo Station. That station is located about an hour away from Seoul station by public transport.

The slowest among these is the Mugunghwa train, which takes roughly six hours and departs from Yongsan Station.

Although the departure stations all differ from one another, ITX, SRT and Mugunghwa all arrive at Busan Station.

Try to avoid the 'non-reserved standing room ticket' as this type of ticket allows you to take a seat only if one is open, but if there isn't you will be standing for the duration of the ride, which can be really uncomfortable and exhausting.

Airplane (to Gimhae International Airport in Busan)

You can also fly from Seoul to Busan. There are about 30 flights a day with more or less 10 minutes between each flight. You can find schedules and prices on Jeju Air or Air Seoul. The flight duration from Seoul to Busan is about one hour.

If you're looking for the best option to catch a flight from Seoul to Busan, consider departing from Gimpo Airport rather than Incheon Airport. Not only is Gimpo Airport located in Seoul, but it usually offers domestic flights. However, if you're landing at Incheon Airport and are getting a flight to Busan on the same day, departing from Incheon will save you time.

It is not easy to predict the exact price of the plane tickets, as prices vary depending on airlines, seasons, days of the week, times, and where you buy the ticket from. However, if you're lucky, you might find a plane ticket that is cheaper than a KTX train ticket.

Flights from both Incheon International Airport and Gimpo Airport arrive at Busan International Airport Gimhae.

. . . .

Tip: Be careful where you buy your tickets from. Although sometimes third-party websites may be cheaper than the official airline website or the local travel agency, always make sure to check their reputation and reviews.

Intercity Express bus Dongseoul - Busan

Another option to get from Seoul to Busan is the Intercity Express bus departing from Seoul Gyeongbu Express Bus Terminal (Gangnam) and Dongseoul Bus Terminal. The estimated travel time is four hours.

You can purchase your ticket on the departure date at the ticket counter. There are also two options to choose from: 'Economy,' or 'Excellent' which is a bus with larger seats and only three seats in each row. For a return ticket in the 'Economy' class, the estimated cost would be around 50,000 KRW, and the 'Excellent' class ticket price around 75,000 KRW.

If you prefer booking your ticket online, you can do that here: https://txbuse.t-money.co.kr/ or here https://www.kobus.co.kr/mrs/satschc.do

Prices and schedules may also vary according to time, day and season.

Bus schedule: https://www.kobus.co.kr/oprninf/alcninqr/oprnAlcnPage.do

Source: https://www.kobus.co.kr

Getting around

To get around Busan, you can use their reliable public transport system, get a taxi, or rent a car yourself. Busan only has four metro lines which makes the city easy to navigate. All the stations are announced in Korean and English, sometimes even Japanese and Chinese. The bus stops all have screens displaying information about the incoming buses in Korean and English. Arrival times are available on the navigation apps for most buses and subways as well as transfer information.

Friday

4 pm: DAH Museum 뮤지엄 다

Located in the center of Busan, you'll find the DAH Museum. DAH is a digital art museum attracting locals as well as tourists with its vibrant and interactive art exhibitions. It's the perfect location for taking photos. There is also has a café inside so that you can savor a cup of Americano while appreciating the vivid displays of lights and colors.

20, Centum seo-ro, Haeundae-gu, Busan
부산 해운대구 센텀서로 20
Centum City Station 센텀시티역, Exit 6
(Busan line 2)

7 pm: Sunset Dadaepo Beach

Dadaepo Beach (다대포해변공원) is located in the west of Busan and attracts people with its beautiful white sand. It is the perfect place for families and people who enjoy water sports like paddleboarding and kiteboarding. Here you can take a walk along the sea, get some beautiful pictures of the scenery, and listen to your favorite BTS songs with your feet in the sand thinking of Jimin.

On February 7th, Jimin uploaded a vlog titled "160107 지민" to the BANGTANTV YouTube channel. In the video, he is taking a walk down Dadaepo Beach with his brother. In the vlog, he makes a wish that he and the members become famous. Little did he know that they would soon become the biggest boy band in the world and the first Korean group to be nominated for a Grammy. He also wished for his members and ARMY to stay happy and healthy.

The sunset at this beach is stunning, presumably why Jimin said they came here to watch it. You can end your day looking out at the romantic nature and wishing for your future, the way Jimin did. Who knows, perhaps yours will come true, too.

(Depending on what time of the year you come, the time at which the sun sets varies. I recommend you check the exact time beforehand!)

Fun fact: When the free BTS concert BTS Yet To Come in Busan concert was held in October 2022, they had a BTS themed light display at this beach.

692, Dadae-ro, Saha-gu, Busan
부산 사하구 다대로 692
Dadaepo Beach Station 다대포해수욕장역,
Exit 6 (Busan line 1)

#SNS

Saturday

7 am: Sunrise at Haedong Yonggungsa Temple 해동용궁사

Stop at the Haedong Yonggungsa Temple (해동용궁사) for one of the most breathtaking sunrises in Korea. Located in the northeast corner of Busan, the temple opens at 5 a.m. and is free of charge. Be careful on rainy days as the stone stairs can be quite slippery!

86, Yonggunggil, Gijang-eup, Gijang-gun, Busan 부산 기장군 기장읍 용궁길 86

no subway

Bus lines 1001, 139, 100, 185

280, Haeundaehaebyeon-ro, Haeundae-gu, Busan

부산 해운대구 해운대해변로 280

Haeundae Station 해운대역, Exit 5 (Busan line 2)

11 am: Soak up the sun in Haeundae

The famous Haeundae Beach (해운대 해수욕장) is considered one of the best beaches in Korea, and walking along the 1.5 km long white-sand beach is an experience you shouldn't miss out on. Surrounded by skyscrapers, the coastline and skyline views are stunning both day and night. You can also grab a bite on the Haeundae Beach promenade, which serves Korean and international cuisine.

2 pm: Breathtaking view via Sky Capsule 스카이캡슐

An attraction you can't find elsewhere in Korea but only in Busan is the 'Sky Capsule.' It is an elevated railway that operates 10 meters (approx 32 feet) above the ground. The colorful cars are an eye catcher, and the train gives its passengers a breathtaking view over the ocean. Although you can buy tickets on-site, it is highly recommended that you book your tickets in advance because they can sell out.

Sky Capsule

Gwangalli Beach

You can book your tickets online at www. bluelinepark.com/eng/skyCapsuleFare. do

116, Cheongsapo-ro, Haeundae-gu, Busan 부산 해운대구 청사포로 116
Centum City Station 센텀시티역, Exit 6 (Busan line 2)

5 pm: To the (food) market

As a port town, Busan is known for the vast variety and quality of its seafood. If you're a seafood lover, do not miss out on Jagalchi Market (자갈치시장), also known as Korea's largest seafood market. Not only is it popular among Koreans, but it is also a well-visited destination for tourists from all over the world.

The market is in Nampodong, located along the seaside with colorful parasols to catch your attention. The market is composed of an outdoor and indoor area. The lively and busy atmosphere of the outdoor market contrasts with the modern indoor area and new shops. Have a browse of the shops, and the merchants are on hand to talk to you and invite you to their stalls. Enjoy a dish of fresh fish while appreciating the view over the sea.

If seafood is not for you, consider Gukje Market (국제시장). Inside Gukje Market, you'll find everything you need, whether it's clothes, household goods, souvenirs, or delicious Korean food.

52, Jagalchihaean-ro, Jung-gu, Busan
부산 중구 자갈치해안로 52
Jagalchi Station 자갈치역, Exit 10 (Busan line 1)

---

7 pm: Watch the Sunset at Gwangalli

Wrap up your day with a stroll along Gwangalli Beach (광안리해수욕장). The 1.4 km long beach is known for its animated beachfront and gorgeous views.

One of the most popular beaches in Busan loved by the younger crowd. The cafés and pubs overlooking the sea and the variety of restaurants offering cuisines from all around the world make it a perfect dinner spot to enjoy the sunset.

By night, the iconic Gwangalli bridge may remind you of Jimin's soulful ballad as you watch the boats swaying peacefully on the sea, the bridge beautifully lit, creating an unforgettable view.

In the summer months on most Saturday nights, drone shows are held over Gwangalli Beach, twice a night at 8pm and 10pm, weather permitting. You can watch hundreds of drones fly out over the ocean and form images and words in the sky and listen to the crowd ooh and ahh over them as well. You may remember these shows if you've enjoyed a BTS concert online and now you can see them in person.

219, Gwanganhaebyeon-ro, Suyeong-gu, Busan 부산 수영구 광안해변로 219

Gamcheon Culture Village

Gamcheon Culture Village

Gwangan Station 광안역, Exit 5 (Busan line 2)

Sunday

10 am : Gamcheon Culture Village 감천문화마을

Your weekend trip to Busan wouldn't be complete without visiting the Gamcheon Culture Village. Nicknamed the 'Machu Picchu of Busan,' this charming little village is a must-see. Located in the foothills of a coastal mountain, the village was built in staircase fashion to ensure no house blocks another's view. The colorful houses and narrow alleyways full of beautiful murals and sculptures make you feel like you've just entered a different world. There is a rooftop platform with a beautiful view over the village and the sea, and there are stores where you can buy fun souvenirs. It first became a popular point of interest for tourists in 2009 when students chose to give the neighborhood a colorful makeover. Art can be found everywhere on stairs, on walls, doors, etc.

In May 2021, a mural in the Gamcheon Cultural Village was created for the two members native to Busan. Entering the main entrance of the village, follow the path to the artwork. It's a big portrait of Jimin and Jung Kook holding roses, next to which is a planet and a fox sitting on the moon, in reference to 'The Little Prince' and Jimin's song "Serendipity".

Busan Citizen Park

Busan Citizen Park

To get to the village, it's easiest to get on the town shuttle bus either from Goejeong station (괴정역) Exit 6, Sahagu (사하구) lines 1 or 1-1, or Toseong Station (토성동역) Exit 6 for Sahagu 1-1, Seogu (서구) lines 2 and 2-2. Get off at Gamjeong Elementary School/Gamcheon village (감정초등학교/감천문화마을). Once off the bus, there will be people waiting to guide you towards the entrance of the village. There is also a very helpful tourist information center in case you are looking for more detailed guidance on navigating the neighborhood.

About half an hour's bus ride from this village is the Song Marine Cable Car (송도해상케이블카), the perfect stop for anyone who loves a good view. The cable car takes you from Songdo Beach to Annam Park, over the open sea. You can choose between a regular car or the Crystal Cruise with its transparent floor. Although this is not a BTS related spot, it's worth a visit.

203, Gamnae 2-ro, Saha-gu, Busan
부산 사하구 감내2로 203
no subway
Bus lines 11, 87, 103, 134, 190

#MadeByARMY

1 pm: Busan Citizen Park 부산시민공원

This park was established with the themes of 'Memory, Culture, Pleasure, Nature and Participation' and lays out a pleasant environment. The park itself is beautiful and makes for a relaxing walk. Especially on sunny days, I would suggest you unwind here while enjoying the picturesque scenery.

In June 2019, BTS held some of their Muster 'Magic Shop' in Busan. In his free time, V must have taken some time to explore the area because on June 15th, he uploaded photos of himself holding an umbrella in this park. To get to the spot where V was standing, walk towards the pavilion (시민마루). Each entrance has a map for reference and the park is not too big, so it's easy to find. They drew footsteps on the ground to mark the exact spot where V stood for his photo.

Beomjeon-dong, Busanjin-gu, Busan
부산 부산진구 범전동
Bujeon Station 부전역, Exit 7 (Busan line 1)

#SNS

Busan Asiad Auxiliary Stadium
부산아시아드주경기장 보조경기장

Located near the Busan Citizen Park is the Busan Asiad Auxiliary Stadium, where BTS held part of their 5th Muster 'Magic Shop'. The Busan Asiad Main Stadium was originally built for the 2002 Asian Games and later used as the site for the 2002 FIFA World Cup. The Auxiliary Stadium is a smaller size next to the Main Stadium. One of the most memorable aspects of this show was

Busan Asiad Auxiliary Stadium

the unique construction of the stage: made to resemble the ARMY logo. There was a main stage in the middle with the crowd on either side and a smaller stage wrapping around the entire venue to give BTS and ARMY a way to see each other from all possible angles. This show was especially meaningful to Jung Kook and Jimin, as they got to perform in their hometown. This was also the venue for their recent free concert titled BTS Yet To Come in Busan to promote Busan's bid for the 2030 World Expo. The concert attracted an audience of about 52,000 people from all over the world.

1342, Geoje-dong, Yeonje-gu, Busan
부산 연제구 거제동 1342
Sports Complex Station 종합운동장역, Exit 9 (Busan line 3)

#Concert

3 pm: Magnate 메그네이트

A must for ARMY in Busan is definitely a visit to Magnate Café (메그네이트), which is run by Jimin's father. Outside the café is a large parking lot, and the building has a rustic design. Inside, it is a rather spacious café, with a lot of sunlight thanks to big windows. There are couches you can relax at and tables where you can work, should you be one of the people who enjoy doing their work in a café. At first sight, there

are no obvious signs of BTS, but if you take a closer look, you'll find a shelf with a few of Jimin's hats. In 2022, the famous artist Lee K painted a Jimin portrait and gifted it to Jimin's father, who placed it inside the cafe. Also, their signature drink is a 'Purple Ade,' a visually pleasing drink that reminds you of BTS, since they have made that the representative color for them and ARMY.

If you plan to come here after visiting the Busan Citizen Park, it will take you around 40 to 50 minutes by bus. Depending on your timing, you can either take a direct bus (numbers 83 or 83-1) or have to transfer in between. The bus stop varies according to where you are in the park, so use a map navigation service to find the closest available bus stop.

Magnate

Magnate

135, Jinnam-ro, Nam-gu, Busan
부산 남구 진남로 135
Motgol Station 못골역, Exit 4 (Busan line 2)

#DailyLife

4 pm: 'Bunezia' Busan's Venezia 부네치아

Another tourist attraction to consider while in Busan is 'Bunezia' at Jangnim Port. This old transformed port located in Western Busan, an area that is not as popular amongst tourists as Eastern Busan, has only recently gained popularity. Nicknamed the 'Venice of Busan,' its colorful buildings serve as a very unique and trendy photo locations not easily found elsewhere in Korea.

There is a food and drink court as well as souvenir shops if you need a break.

72, Jangnim-ro 93 beongil, Saha-gu, Busan 부산 사하구 장림로 93번길 72
Jangnim Station 장림역, Exit 3 (Busan line 1)

Other Locations in Busan

If you have extra time during your stay in Busan, then here are some other locations to highlight that may not quite fit into a 48 hour time period.

Confio 콘피오

This is the café that V met with his actor friend Park Bogum to drink melon juice and chat together. BTS was in Busan for

Confio

their '2019 Muster: MAGIC SHOP' and Park Bogum was in town to film a movie. The owner of the café, who is a fan of both celebrities, posted on social media that evening about how she couldn't believe two of her idols had come to her café and played with her cat. She posted on social media a photo of their autographs that they gave her.

This café is less than a 10 minute walk from Busan Citizen Park. The table where V and Bogum sat is the one closest to the front window. There is a painting that represents the scene of the two of them together inside the door to the café. There are also other paintings and posters dedicated to V and BTS. This includes a stand with the latest BTS albums and the two glasses used to serve V and Bogum their refreshing melon juices. The staff is extremely welcoming: Confio offers good food quality and price, and if you come later in the day you might find the café is full with regular patrons. It is definitely a café worth taking the time to visit.

33, Seongji-ro 8 beongil, Busanjin-gu, Busan 부산 부산진구 성지로 8번길 33 Yangjeong Station 양정역, Exit 3 (Busan line 1)

Gopchang Salon Yeontangui
곱창쌀롱 연탄구이

Also near Busan Citizen Park and Confio café is Gopchang Salon Yeontangui, a beef tripe restaurant that has turned into a BTS fan zone. This restaurant is one that Jung Kook frequents when he comes home to Busan. He has left his signature here, referring to the owner as 'uncle' and the seat he used has also been turned into its own designated space. Fans have donated posters, photos, acrylic stands, keyrings and every kind of BTS themed item to this restaurant and the owner is kind enough to display them all. Even the outside clearly displays how ARMY friendly the restaurant is.

The restaurant opens at 5pm but stays open until late. Most popular are its set menus. It's a good idea to come with at least one other person since options serve 2-3 people. You can get gopchang, makchang, galbi and chicken's feet here, and all meals will be served with the proper Korean side dishes (banchan) such as radish, lettuce leaves, garlic, ssamjang paste, onions and salad. Also the side dishes of steamed egg, tofu and seaweed soup come for free. The portions are generous and since the meat is cooked over a briquette fire it is extra tasty and leaves little wonder why this restaurant is a favorite for Jung Kook.

44, Dongpyeong-ro 223 beongil, Yeonji-dong, Busanjin-gu, Busan

부산 부산진구 연지동 동평로 223번길 44

Bujeon Station 부전역, Exit 1 (Busan line 1)

Gopchang Salon Yeontangui

Oryukdo Skywalk

Busan Museum of Art and Space Lee Ufan 부산시립미술관

This museum seems to be a favorite for BTS's leader, RM. He has shared three of his visits here on social media, the first in June 2019 when he toured the Space Lee Ufan permanent exhibit and left a message in the visitor book saying, "I enjoyed it, I liked 'From Winds.'" He went back in May 2020, this time to see contemporary Korean artist Kim Chong-hak's work and left the message, "I hope we can overcome the hard times together with Kim Chong-hak's state of 'Rhythmic Vitality.'" Then on Valentine's day in 2022 RM posted a series of photos on his personal instagram of his latest visit to the Busan Museum of Art, this time he focused on the exhibit 'Christian Boltanski: 4.4' by the French artist of the same name who passed away in 2021.

Oryukdo Skywalk

This museum has a main building and a separate permanent space for the Space Lee Ufan exhibit. The museum also contains a café, art shop, auditorium and spaces designed for entertaining and educating children. There used to be entrance fees to both spaces in the past, but recently they permitted free entry. It is best to check their website https://art. busan.go.kr to see if you will need to pay to enter. You can also find out what the latest collections are on exhibit and any upcoming events here too.

The museum is open every day except Mondays and public holidays.

Oryukdo Skywalk

Opening hours: 10am-6pm (last entry 5pm)

58, APEC-ro, Haeundae-gu, Busan
부산 해운대구 APEC로 58
Bexco Station 벡스코역, Exit 5 (Busan line 2)

Oryukdo Skywalk 오륙도 스카이워크

Oryukdo is a series of six islands on the south-east coast of Busan. 'Oryukdo' literally translates to '5-6 islands' as at high tide there are five islands visible, and at low tide there are six. Jimin came to Oryukdo in 2015 and made a vlog for ARMY in which he explains the name of Oryukdo. There is the Oryukdo Skywalk here as well, which is a glass-floored walkway that goes over part of the ocean and allows for great views of the Busan

sea, the Oryukdo islands and of the city of Busan. It is free to the public and an easy 30 minute bus ride from most parts of Busan. You can type in 'Oryukdo Skywalk' into your navigation app to find the best methods of transportation to get here. Also in this area are various trails and hiking paths for those who feel adventurous or want to take in more of that ocean air.

Open Monday-Sunday
Hours: 9am-6pm

137, Oryukdo-ro, Nam-gu, Busan
부산 남구 오륙도로 137
no subway
Bus lines 24, 27, 131

HOPE WORLD

KPOP STAR GWANGJU
케이팝
스타거

K-Pop Star Street

Weekend Trip

Gwangju

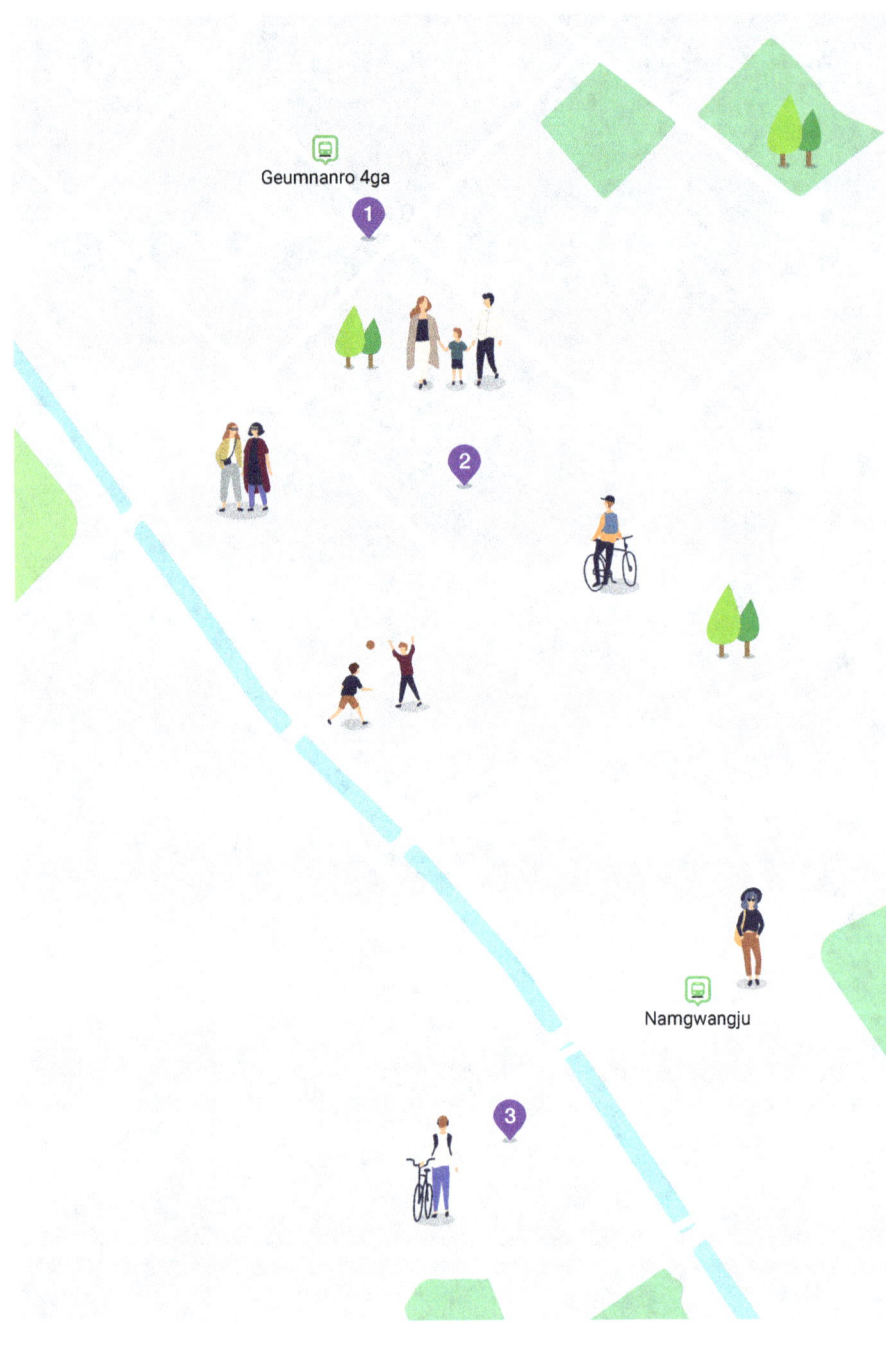

Geumnanro 4ga

Namgwangju

1 Joydance Plugin Music Academy
2 K-Pop Star Street
3 Penguin Village

Gwangju
광주

Gwangju - explore the hometown of j-hope

Gwangju is located in the southwest of Korea in the Jeolla province, often referred to as Jeollanamdo. This area is very influential to in Korea for its history, culture and the temperament of its people. People from Gwangju, or Jeolla in general, are often characterized to be very friendly and laid back. This part of the country is also known to be very progressive in politics and is referred to as the birthplace of democracy for the historic May 18 Democratic Uprising. There are monuments, information guides and memorials to this event throughout the city. While not directly related to BTS, we do recommend visiting the Asia Culture Complex, the 5.18 Archives, the May 18th National Cemetery and the Jeonsil 245 building. It is absolutely best to learn about the event before going to Gwangju or you'll miss out on the context of this incredible city.

Other than the significance of its place in Korean history, Gwangju has a strong art and culture scene. And since it is in Jeolla, Gwangju is often referred to as the food capital of Korea, for its excellent culinary scene. But if nature is more your thing, then there is the Mudeungsan National Park (무등산국립공원) with easy access to the Damyang Bamboo Forest (담양죽녹원) and

Gwangju Station

Boseong Green Tea Fields (대한다원) too. Damyang Bamboo Forest is designated as a 'Slow City' for its eco-friendly environment and local food culture. Also worth mentioning are two internationally renown Buddhist temples, Baekyangsa, where chef/nun made famous vegan temple cuisine and Hwaensa, where RM spent a night of Templestay.

Of course, Gwangju is most famous to ARMY as the birthplace and hometown for BTS's sunshine, j-hope. He grew up here with his family and beloved dog, Micky, went to school and learned street dance in Gwangju. To this day his family still lives in Gwangju and j-hope goes back to visit as often as he can. This combined with his love of the area and

Gwangju

acknowledging his roots in songs like "Chicken Noodle Soup," "Ma City " and "Paldogangsan," make Gwangju a must visit for ARMY.

Getting to Gwangju

There are various methods of getting to Gwangju from Seoul, but the main options are by public transportation either KTX train or Intercity Express bus.

KTX Train

You can take a KTX train from Yongsan Station to Gwangju Songjeong Station with an average travel time of 2hr 35 minutes. Trains usually depart every hour, but it is still wise to book a ticket ahead

Gwangju Station

of time. Tickets can be purchased either online through the Korean rail website (https://www.letskorail.com/ebizbf/EbizbfForeign_pr16100.do?gubun=1), or in person at the station.

Intercity Express Bus

Another option to travel to Gwangju is the Intercity Express bus. Though take note that it is a 3.5 hour journey from Seoul without traffic, so not the most efficient for a short trip. The bus will depart from Seoul Central City Bus Terminal and arrive at Gwangju Bus Terminal.

Buses are operated by several private companies so seats and schedules differ. You can purchase your ticket on the departure date at the ticket counter.

There are also two options to choose from: 'Economy,' or 'Excellent.' For a one-way ticket in the 'Economy' class, the estimated cost would be around 19,800 KRW, and in the 'Excellent' class the ticket price would be around 29,300 KRW.

If you prefer booking your ticket online, you can do that here: https://txbuse.t-money.co.kr/ or here https://www.kobus.co.kr/mrs/satschc.do

Prices and schedule times may vary according to time, day and season.

Note: there are two different bus terminals in Gwangju depending on your destination. Please be sure that you are at the right one.

Joydance Plugin Music Academy

Joydance Plugin Music Academy
조이댄스 플러그인뮤직아카데미

Kick off your day trip to Gwangju with a visit to Joydance Plugin Music Academy. Among many other idols, this is the dance school j-hope attended. The academy markets itself as a "professional institution for education of applied dance and music" that has expanded throughout Korea ever since its opening in 2003. Their main goal is paving the way for students to become professional performers.

The 'Fan Zone' on the first floor leads you into a foyer area with a TV monitor displaying interviews with various Idols from Gwangju, photos and fanart of particular members of groups, and a wall of albums. There is a list of Idols who have been to the academy over the years and under 2010 you can find 'j-hope' listed. Other than a few photos, there is nothing explicitly related to j-hope or BTS here, but there is an exciting atmosphere as students attending dance and music lessons are always coming and going. In the past a video of j-hope's old audition tape to BigHit used to be displayed, though nowadays it does not seem to be there anymore, but it is worth remembering that this is where the process for BTS's j-hope's debut began.

This music academy is located right next to Geumnamro 4 Station (금남로4역) on Line 1. If you come up Exit 1, the building is around the corner. The public is allowed to access the first floor 'Fan Zone' but the other floors are dedicated to members and should be left alone out of respect and privacy.

. . . .

For reference: this is a video where you can see the "Fan Zone" right when you enter the building : *https://www.youtube. com/watch?v=ti0dlNF0L6k*

3F, 185 Chungangro, Dong-gu, Gwangju
광주 동구 중앙로 185 3F
Geumnamno 4ga Station 금남로4가역, Exit 1 (Gwangju line 1)

'Fanzone 03' Fan Art Exhibit

'Fanzone 03' Fan Art Exhibit

'Fanzone 03' Fan Art Exhibit

If you travel by subway to the Joydance Plugin Music Academy, then inside Geumnamo 4 station you should also find another K-Pop fan zone dedicated to fanart. Between the platform and the exits there is a section of the station reserved for shops and restaurants. Exit 1 will take you towards the Dance Academy, but between exit 1 and exit 2 you will come across a creative section with a row of booths set up, a small stage for busking, and a BTS mural on a pillar. It is not at all advertised so you have to know it's there to find it, but this makes the discovery it all the more rewarding.

This 'Fan Zone' exists because in 2021, to promote the 'K-Pop Star Street,' created by Gwangju City for tourism, a contest was held for BTS fanart, with entries open to fans both in Korea and internationally. Forty-five pieces of art are exhibited here, including the contest winners that cover art forms from calligraphy, digital art, paintings and embroidery. Though a large section is dedicated to BTS, further along there is another part with fanart for other Idols including Blackpink, IU and TXT. As this isn't an area with lots of foot traffic, it's nice to take your time to appreciate each artwork and consider the time, effort and love that was put into them by the fans. To see all that love recognized by a city is extra heart-warming. As it is free to access and close to other notable K-Pop zones, there is no reason not to visit this space.

Geumnamno 4(sa)-ga Dong-gu, Gwangju
광주 동구 금남로 4가
Geumnamno 4ga Station 금남로4가역, Exit 1 (Gwangju line 1)

K-Pop Star Street 케이팝스타의 거리

Only a short walk away from the Music Academy, you'll find 'Chungjangno,' a shopping district reminiscent of Myeong-dong in Seoul. This busy shopping street includes all the brands you'd also find in Myeongdong, and leads you to the K-Pop Star Street, which seems to be a continuously evolving, ongoing project. To reach this street, walk straight until you see the FILA store, turn right, and next to the post office, you'll see the huge HOPE World mural.

As you walk into K-Pop Star Street, you'll see murals on garage doors dedicated to various artists, including j-hope's "Chicken Noodle Soup." As part of a birthday project, fans had a 'j-hope bench' made with art from his Hope World music videos used to decorate it. j-hope came here in 2022 to take pictures and share them on social media. Next to the bench is a 'HOPE' statue that has 21,800 names of fans from 148 countries. As thanks,

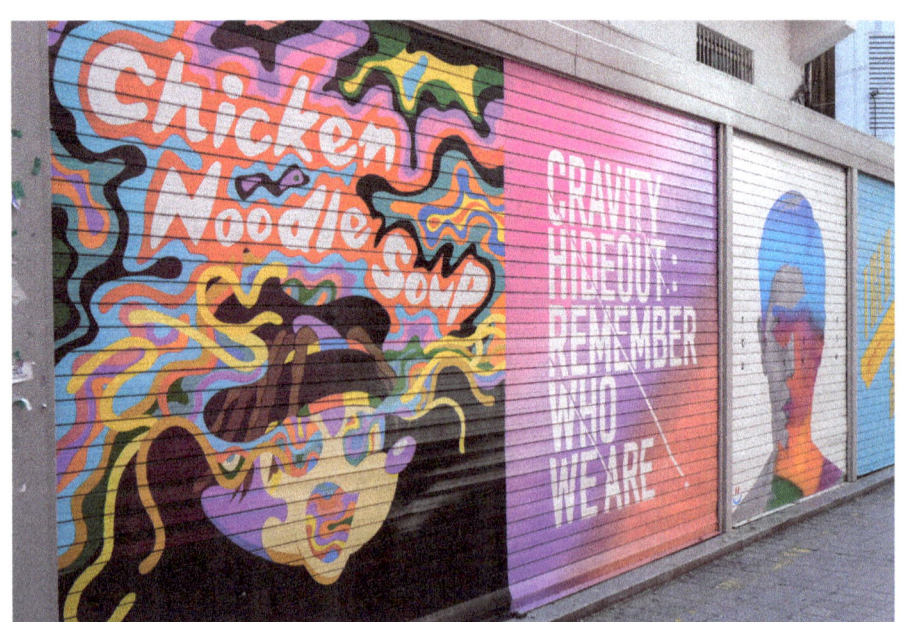

K-Pop Star Street

j-hope left his signature and a message that is on a plaque on the statue. The handwritten message reads: "I'm touched to see the messages from fans all over the world!! I'll continue to work hard so that I don't feel embarrassed by the fans' love. Thank you."

There are other benches, panels and displays for other artists in this area too. You can find handprint molds of various idols and groups, plus a collection of different fan lightsticks, including the iconic Armybomb. Be on the lookout for a mural for the Megan the Stallion remix of "Butter" in this area as well. It's a charming area to walk through but can

K-Pop Star Street

get busy, so if you want to take photos without crowds try coming before 10am.

There is also a HOPE statue put up :

Chungjangno 3(sam)-ga, Dong-gu, Gwangju 광주 동구 충장로 3가
Geumnamno 4ga Station 금남로4가역, Exit 1 (Gwangju line 1)

Penguin Village 펭귄마을

Another popular destination in Gwangju is the Penguin Village. You'll find a lot of cute photo spots in the village, which is named after the way the elderly with knee pain walk. The area is filled with artists

HOPE statue

Penguin Village

selling handmade items, making it feel like an outdoor arts and crafts museum.

While getting lost in the small alleys, you'll find two paintings of j-hope on the wall, and another cute photospot dedicated to his birthday. This painting was made in February 2020 with support from his Chinese Fans as a birthday event. The murals are two different versions of j-hope from his "Outro: Ego" music video and highlight his sweet, angelic nature.

7, Cheonbyeonjwa-ro 446 beongil, Nam-gu, Gwangju 광주 남구 천변좌로 446번길 7 Namgwangju Station 남광주역, Exit 3 (Gwangju line 1)

Cheongchun Balsan Village
청춘 발산마을

For j-hope's birthday in 2021, Chinese fans fundraised for an expansive mural of the star to be created within the Youth Balsan Village. The mural was created February 16th, in time for his birthday on the 18th. The mural measures 12 meters wide and 3.5 meters high and is done in a similar art style to that of the Penguin Village mural, probably as the same fan group organized both murals. This one has j-hope in two iconic outfits: one the black Dior piece he performed "Outro:Tear" on the 'Love Yourself: Speak Yourself' tour. He is pictured sitting on a multicolored version of the world, looking up. The

Cheongchun Balsan Village

other is also a Dior outfit, this time the full red suit j-hope performed "Trivia 起: Just Dance" in the same concert tour. He is holding a red mic and looking out at an imagined crowd. In the center, in rainbow letters reads 'HOPE WORLD 1994 0218' to mark his birthdate.

In the 1970s, Balsan Village used to be near the Jeonnam Textile Factory, and so many of the factory workers (a largely female workforce) ended up living in the Balsan Village area as it was a cheap option. Overtime, however, the industrial workforce changed and the textile factory closed, meaning more and more of the houses were abandoned, leaving only the elderly behind, and the village began to fall into disrepair. In 2015 the

Cheongchun Balsan Village

Hyundai Motor Group teamed up with the group Public Prism to revitalize the neighborhood with workshops, art and new businesses. Now the Balsan Village is a popular date spot for young couples.

To get here you will need to catch a bus which will drop you at the Balsan Village entrance. You can walk through the area, and when you see a set of colorful steps (all 108 of them), you will need to climb them. At the top is a street with various murals, and if you journey down the left you will quickly come across the j-hope birthday murals.

12-16, Cheonbyeonjwa-ro, Seo-gu, Gwangju 광주 서구 천변좌로 12-16 Yangdongsijang Station 양동시장역, Exit 4 (Gwangju line 1)

Cheongchun Balsan Village

Appendix

Acknowledgements

This book came to be out of our love for BTS and the shared community of ARMY. The love we felt through the music, artistry and every episode of Run BTS! – not to mention the Lives – has inspired us to give back. It is our hope that this guide helps ARMY (re)visit locations previously seen only on screens and to relive those beautiful moments that have made us laugh, cry and heal.

As you make new memories on your visit to Korea, through the purchase of this guide, you are also giving back to the community as a portion of its profits will be donated to various ARMY efforts around the world. Announcements will be made annually via social media.

This book could not have happened without its many iterations in writing and design. Its look required the vision of Sanghwa Lee. Bora K shared her passion on every page, having traveled far and wide with photographer, Matt Ha. Jennifer Roe came in to expand our written and photo coverage post-pandemic as changes became inevitable. Thanks to travel guru, Jil Weyland for itineraries and additional coverage in Busan. To Keri who did another round of reading when we couldn't see the trees from the forest.

In our first foray into producing this book, human error will be likely and places will change. Please feel free to contact us and let us know.

yougenmedia@naver.com

Please use these pages as a travel journal. Moments to remember.

Dream

Shine

Smile

Tomorrow is another day.

Smile at the sky.

Wherever you go, there you are.

It does not matter how slowly you go as long as you do not stop